Lind Corley
Londm
22. iii.97

A

TO SPEAK FOR OURSELVES
THE LONDON SYMPHONY ORCHESTRA

TO SPEAK FOR OURSELVES

The London Symphony Orchestra

Edited by
ALAN SMYTH

With photographs by
PAUL KATZ

WILLIAM KIMBER · LONDON

First published in 1970 by
WILLIAM KIMBER & CO. LIMITED
22a Queen Anne's Gate London, S.W.1

© The London Symphony Orchestra 1970

SBN 7183 0491 8

MADE AND PRINTED IN GREAT BRITAIN BY PURNELL AND SONS, LTD.
PAULTON (SOMERSET) AND LONDON

CONTENTS

	page
EDITOR'S NOTE	7
INTRODUCTION	8

PART ONE

ANDRE PREVIN,
Principal Conductor of the L.S.O.   13

PART TWO

THE STRINGS

JOHN GEORGIADIS, Leader of the L.S.O.	26
WILLIAM BENHAM, Violin	37
SAMUEL ARTIS, Second Violin	47
ALEXANDER TAYLOR, Principal Viola	51
DOUGLAS CUMMINGS, Principal Cello	58
JACK LONG, Cello	63
MARTIN ROBINSON, Cello	66
STUART KNUSSEN, Principal Double Bass	68

PART THREE

WOODWIND

PETER LLOYD, Principal Flute	79
ROGER LORD, Principal Oboe	82
GERVASE DE PEYER, Principal Clarinet	87
RONALD MOORE, Clarinet	94
ROGER BIRNSTINGL, Principal Bassoon	99

PART FOUR

THE HORNS AND BRASS

	page
IVAN DAVID GRAY, Principal Horn	113
HOWARD SNELL, Principal Trumpet	123
DENIS WICK, Principal Trombone	129
FRANK MATHISON, Bass Trombone	140
JOHN FLETCHER, Tuba	143

PART FIVE

THE TIMPANI, PERCUSSION AND HARP

KURT HANS GOEDICKE, Principal Timpani	157
JAMES HOLLAND, Principal Percussion	165
OSIAN ELLIS, Principal Harp	174
MEMBERS OF THE L.S.O.	184
INDEX	187

EDITOR'S NOTE

To Speak For Ourselves originated from a suggestion to the London Symphony Orchestra from Mr. William Kimber that an interesting book could be produced if the orchestra would be willing to co-operate in producing a volume which would show the orchestra at work by combining action photographs with a text derived from a cross-section of members of the orchestra describing their musical and private lives in their own words.

Twenty-one of the musicians and their conductor have been interviewed, allowed to talk freely about their playing and private lives. The chapters have in the main been left in dialogue form and must be read as colloquial conversation, and not as edited prose. The players were selected as being representative of their instrumental sections within the orchestra, and not for their wit or musical punditry. In the happy event, however, they are articulate and often amusing.

Some I visited in their homes, others I spoke to in my London flat, in the musicians' bar of the Royal Festival Hall, on trains, aircraft, and in hotel rooms; in fact anywhere where the location of this much-travelling orchestra allowed me to get at them. I had prepared a list of questions for each, but it was never necessary to use these as, talking to my colleagues and friends in this way, conversation flowed of its own easy accord.

We hope that these twenty-two interviews with musicians from the L.S.O. present a cumulative picture, a feeling of what it is like today to be in one of the great symphony orchestras of the world.

INTRODUCTION

At the turn of the century in London, orchestral performances were a comparatively rare occurrence, and musicians depended for their living on theatres, restaurants and music halls—with symphony concerts taking first place artistically, but decidedly second place when financial considerations were taken into account. A great orchestra was the Queen's Hall Orchestra run by Mr. Henry Wood, later to become Sir Henry Wood and to be known amongst musicians forever as 'Timbers'. Even to be a member of the Queen's Hall Orchestra, however, could not offer a secure living in itself to any musician. And it was the pattern of their lives to play in many places, many types of music and for many employers. Arranging one's diary with conflicting engagements must have been a nightmare. It was a nightmare which gave rise to the deputy system whereby a musician could send a deputy engaged by himself to cover any odd rehearsals when he could not be present. Henry Wood hated this system and in 1903 made the musicians an offer. He could not have known how far-reaching the results of his offer were to be. It led to the formation of at least two major symphony orchestras in London, and radically changed the whole pattern of concert giving. The offer was a simple one: a flat rate of £100 a year providing that the Queen's Hall Orchestra had the first call on the players' services. This meant—no deputies. There is no doubt that the offer was made with the interests of artistic standards in mind. But Henry Wood misjudged his musicians—he failed to understand their mood. The result was a massive walk-out of the players from his orchestra. At least fifty players left and adopted an idea of four of them: three horn players—Borsdorf, Busby and van der Meerschen—with John Solomon, the trumpeter. Their idea was to found the London Symphony Orchestra. Sir Henry's offer must have made them feel all the more aware of their frustrations in not having control of their affairs financially as well as artistically: the new orchestra would run itself, that was the first principle; the musicians would have a say in everything. Alongside this the most important principle of all was decided upon. The orchestra would only be worthwhile were it to insist at all times on the highest standards. The first move was a bold and dramatic one. The engagement of Hans Richter from Germany for the opening concert—

8

this to be held at The Queen's Hall, where the old orchestra was so well known—on June 9th, 1904. Contemporary reports of the performances contain words like 'brilliant' and 'staggering'. It must have been a great afternoon's concert, because the orchestra was soon accepting engagements from all over England. The two first principles have certainly been adhered to. The orchestra has always been self-governed and still is today, and its players jealously guard this first principle. Its artistic excellence is now a legend. The L.S.O.'s history includes associations with names such as Richter, Nikisch, Elgar, Joseph Krips, Monteux, Kertesz and Andre Previn, its present principal conductor. No sooner was the orchestra launched in 1904 than it began looking abroad. In spite of the difficulties of arranging foreign trips in those days they nevertheless took place. After two years a trip to Paris, then Antwerp, and in 1912 America and Canada. In more recent years associations with gramophone recording and film music have provided part of the pattern of work of the orchestra. The L.S.O.'s first recording contract was signed in 1920 and long associations since then with famous recording companies have spread the fame of the L.S.O. throughout the musical world.

Born out of a mood of revolt against authority, the administrative history of the L.S.O. has had its turbulent moments. Today, although not in revolt, the musicians are noted for a vital and intelligent interest in all of their affairs. The orchestra is still full of colourful personalities —interesting people in their own right, as well as masters of their chosen instruments. They are still arrogantly independent, self-governing in their administration, but utterly subservient to their real masters, the composers of the music they perform.

In nearly seventy years, the London Symphony Orchestra has attained many laurels, in England and abroad. We aim for challenging concerts, and strive for the highest standards which the internationally competitive orchestral situation demands, in all of them. We have won the modern accolade of success, to be dubbed 'the most recorded orchestra'. But, more important, we have won friends all over the world. The L.S.O. is a very complex organization, both in its administration and in its deployment of instrumental talents. Before launching into the conversations with the players themselves, it may be helpful to set down here some of the factual details concerned with the day-to-day running of our orchestra.

Instrumentalists are admitted to the L.S.O. only after most careful selection based on auditions, the reputations of the players, recommendations, 'trial runs' in the orchestra, or a combination of all these. Mistakes with personnel selection are thus very rare. New members buy ten shares each with the company; these are only available to players and are not negotiable; they entitle the holder to attend all L.S.O. meetings, and are usually returned when a member leaves the orchestra.

We normally field a string section of: sixteen first violins; fourteen seconds; twelve violas; ten cellos; and eight basses. On rare occasions, this is reluctantly (on our part) reduced by one desk in each department, for reasons of economy, or orchestral 'balance'. For classical works, we diminish still further at the discretion of the conductor. For instance, Mozart symphonies are usually played with a string strength of 10-8-6-4-2 respectively in each section, but this is by no means a general rule. John Georgiadis is our leader, associated with John Brown. Each string section has a principal and co-principal; one or the other has to be present on each engagement or promotion, except in cases of illness.

We have a fine team of loyal 'extras'—the pick of London's freelance pool, who play for us when needed to fill the places of absent members, or where unfilled vacancies occur. One of the great advantages of organizing music in London is the standard of its freelance musicians, which draws a great deal of music-making here for records, films, radio, T.V., as well as all the concert activities. It is normal for some of the 'extras' to become L.S.O. members later.

We use a system of co-principals for the woodwinds, horns and brass. 'Second' instruments in the woodwinds do not necessarily play 'first' when both the principals are unavoidably absent. A usual arrangement would be for a principal from another London orchestra or a freelance player to be engaged for that occasion. Seconds do, however, often specialise in 'fringe' solo instruments—the E flat clarinet, contrabassoon, alto-flute; at present, the L.S.O. have their own principal positions for the cor anglais (Anthony Camden), piccolo (Lowry Saunders), and bass clarinet (Hale Hambleton). All of these are full members of, and hold shares in, the L.S.O. 'Extras' come in for more of these instruments, and for the rarer use of mandolin, banjo, guitar, saxophone, zither, accordion, Wagner tuba, alpine horn and even sometimes musical saw.

We have five members of the horn section, including the two principals—Ivan David Gray and Anthony Halstead. (High parts are played by horns one and three, low ones by two and four—this has to be borne in mind when booking extra horns.) William Lang and Howard Snell share the first trumpet position; Dennis Wick (trombone) has assistant principal Peter Gane on hand. There is one bass trombone, tuba, timpani and harp. Three members play percussions, often supplemented by a battery of extras.

The intricate problems of day-to-day orchestral personnel management fall safely into the arms of Terry Palmer. His is the responsibility for seeing that we really *are* sitting there when the conductor walks on expecting to conduct us. He telephones extra players, arranges rotas, deals tactfully with us when we display prima donna symptoms. (And he always has plenty of aspirins.) Stephen Rumsey aids and abets Terry, who always has a solution to all problems, fairly earning the tag 'Nanny'.

Danny Liddington is everybody's friend—Danny looks after the orchestral set-up on stage, drives the van and humps the heavier instruments to and from each engagement. Timpani, harps, double basses present special problems, being both very hefty and very fragile. Danny comes into his own on tours abroad, with his specialized knowledge of teamsters' unions, and the holds of various aircraft types. We all rely on him; he is the only one of us who is indispensable.

The L.S.O.'s by now extensive music library is housed in the Royal Albert Hall, tended by Henry Greenwood, himself an ex-member of the L.S.O.'s violin section and therefore unusually familiar with the problems of the playing musician. A complete set of old programmes is stored at the L.S.O.'s offices, along with boardroom minutes, posters and other literature concerned with our own, and other, orchestras, dating back to the L.S.O.'s first appearances in 1904.

The L.S.O.'s administration offices are at 1 Montague Street, in the shadow of the British Museum. They are run by Harold Lawrence, who, in his three years with us, has brought a measure of order and confidence we had not known. His appointment was made by the board.

This board of directors consists of nine playing musicians who are elected for three-year terms by the performing membership, three directors each year. Ultimately, they are responsible to the orchestra for all matters, musical, administrative and financial. They happily delegate administration to the general manager, however, who appoints his staff, and confers with the directors at fortnightly board-meetings. Sub-committees are formed from within the board, to deal with different aspects of the orchestra's life—finance, personnel, chorus, programmes, tours, etc.

The L.S.O. Trust, established in 1963, exists to raise funds to assist our activities in England and abroad, supplementing the subsidies received from private and public funds, notably the Peter Stuyvesant Foundation and Arts Council of Great Britain through the London Orchestral Concerts Board. Without their assistance, our foreign tours would be impossible, so inevitable are the deficits; and our U.K. programmes would have to be fashioned with only box-office considerations in mind. We would surely lose heart in that unthinkable circumstance. Worthwhile concerts are our reason for being.

The L.S.O. Club has a membership of nearly a thousand now. It exists to further our interests as an orchestra, and to encourage closer links between orchestra and audience. It offers its members privilege booking of tickets, attendance at selected rehearsals, evenings of music, talks, social occasions and outings together, along with a monthly bulletin. Some of the members are our most regular patrons, offering encouragement by their enthusiasm and friendliness. We like 'The Club'.

Our chorus is all amateur, in every respect that is except the sound it makes. Under Arthur Oldham they have been making orchestra and audiences alike catch their breath with a new standard of amateur choral singing.

The system works. We have not substantially changed it in nearly seventy years, and we guard it.

'The L.S.O.' is an ever-changing, quite amorphous coterie. It is our privilege to be the custodians of those three initials for our generation as its members, and to foster the interests of them on behalf of London's music. Others will surely do the same in future generations.

ANDRE PREVIN

Principal Conductor of the L.S.O.

A.S.: What is the conductor for?

A.P.: Well, I think first of all for the over-simplified reason of just being the traffic cop; you know—making sure that everyone is playing at the same speed and at the same volume. I have always thought, too, that if there are 85 players, then there are 85 possible interpretations of the piece; and in its own peculiar way, if there are 3,000 people in the audience, then there are 3,000 simultaneous interpretations going on of the piece you are playing. So for good, bad or indifferent, like it or not, you have to detail the responsibility for deciding which interpretation the orchestra is going to play to one man—who makes up their minds for them.

A.S.: What about the merit of an orchestra—does the better group demand more detailed instruction, or does its merit mean that you can give the players more detailed instructions that they can carry out?

A.P.: I suppose a little of both. Do you remember that we've done a couple of concerts which we haven't rehearsed at all, because the material was standard and because the merit of the L.S.O. is so high that, by just paying attention, they can outguess the conductor some nights: on the other hand, very often when I am guest conductor for lesser orchestras, I will settle for certain executions because I know that, however hard they try, they won't improve. With an orchestra like the London Symphony, or the Philadelphia, or the Boston, or whatever, you can ask them to do things that are very virtuoso, which you could not ask from a lesser band.

A.S.: But if you've a great respect for a virtuoso orchestra, might the soloists in this orchestra be allowed more freedom with their own tunes, for instance, or would you be tempted to give them more direction?

A.P.: I would always give them all the freedom they wanted. With our woodwind players—remember when we recorded Scheherazade?— I really made absolutely no suggestions until I found out exactly how they wanted to do it, and then damned few, because if you have great soloists in an orchestra, they should be given as much head as possible.

A.S.: But if there is a point of conflict between the conductor and the players, the players understand that you have the last word?

A.P.: Oh! they don't always understand, but they try!

A.S.: What do you feel about conductor-less orchestras?

A.P.: I've never seen one. I've seen some that appear to be such, but I've never seen one where there was actually no one standing there.

A.S.: Some chamber orchestras are led by the leader. He is the conductor, then, is he?

A.P.: Oh, you mean like Rudolf Barshai, Moscow and all that? Well, that seems to work very well for a specific repertoire. I know very little about that.

A.S.: Do you think that . . .

A.P.: I'm not going to advocate conductor-less orchestras, no matter how you put it!

A.S.: Well, so the conductor is a sort of traffic cop. How do the musicians know what his signs mean?

A.P.: I think by being exposed to his particular kind of conducting for a little while—it takes very little time for even major differences to be ironed out. I was in Philadelphia recently and the Philadelphia Orchestra—which is one of the great orchestras—has that habit of playing almost a full second after the beat—something I thought was very middle-European, but then they are the Philadelphia and they're totally used to this from Ormandy. I finally went kinda mad because I couldn't cope with it any more, and I *begged* them to play at the bottom of the beat, and they in turn could not do it. They said, 'When you're here with us for eight concerts next time, maybe we will, but not for two—it takes us too long.'

Whether the conductor is very precise and easy to follow, or very imprecise and difficult, it doesn't usually take a very good orchestra terribly long to adjust. I don't think there is a greater difference in style possible than—forgive me for being personal but it's the only way I can explain—between Sir John Barbirolli and myself. He had the Houston Orchestra in Texas until three years ago, when I took over from him with immense difference in methods, but, since it's a very good orchestra, it didn't take them longer than maybe half the season to switch over.

A.S.: What aspect of being a conductor appeals to you most? Of course, you have been a performer too, which . . .

A.P.: First of all, the orchestral repertoire is the greatest in the world, and I think the orchestra is the greatest cumulative instrument, with all those marvellous noises it can make. To make good music, first of all, is a marvellous thing, and to make great music with a great orchestra is almost indescribably wonderful—much more so than when playing a solo instrument, which I was used to for a while.

A.S.: Do you ever feel frustrated having to communicate to others how to play?

A.P.: No, not in the least. I would much rather be the middle-man. You see, the thing is that—it's very difficult to say this without sounding pompous—if you're playing great music, I feel that the conductor is responsible directly to the composer for the length of time the piece takes to play. If a piece takes twenty minutes, then for those twenty minutes you really have the composer's wishes and well-being and ambitions in mind, and I think that is a laudable responsibility. Of course, the performers would have that too, but I get back to the fact that the orchestral sound is the one of which I am most fond— much fonder for instance than the sound of the human voice, which I suppose is the most musical and historically pure and all that . . . But I basically think that singers are a dangerous lot and I would much rather concern myself with *playing* musicians.

A.S.: Do you remember the first time you conducted the L.S.O.? What was your impression?

A.P.: Well, it was manifold, in that I was a bit intimidated because— not only was it an orchestra that I had never faced before, which is

*'If you have great soloists in an orchestra,
they should be given as much head as possible.'
Andre Previn and John Georgiadis.*

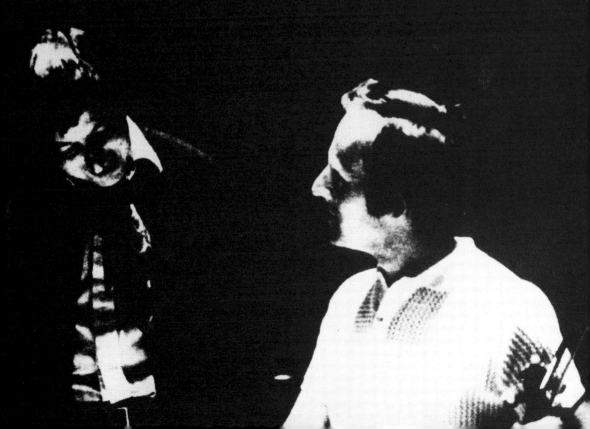

difficult anywhere—but also because the orchestra was so damned good! And then—a small thing I know—but don' forget that having been raised and worked in America all these yea. , I didn't even know the difference in the vocabulary when it came to the technical termin-ology of time values. I didn't know about crotchets and minims and quavers and all that. And this added up to make a rather uneasy beginning, but I thought that the generosity of the orchestra in terms of giving was extraordinary, and it didn't take me long to get used to conducting them.

You know, there was something that happened a little over a year ago that is so apt that it sounds as though it is publicity, and it really isn't. I was on a programme on the B.B.C. called 'Desert Island Discs' with Roy Plomley—do you know that? At the end he said: 'Let me ask you this, Mr. Previn, do you some day want, as an ultimate ambition, the New York Philharmonic, the Philadelphia, the Boston, the Vienna . . . what?'

And I said, with no trace of geographical aptness, but just because I meant it: 'Some day I really would love to have the L.S.O.'

He said 'When?' and I said 'Well, let's say in ten years'.

And then two months later you invited me to become principal conductor. It sounds a bit like a fan magazine, but I had to contain myself not to run around the ceilings when you called.

A.S.: You have been interested in children's concerts?

A.P.: Yes, very. I think children's concerts are very often passed over too quickly. I think that to play music to children in their forma-tive years can either put them off it forever, or get them interested forever, and that to do these concerts helter skelter and not give them a lot of thought, and not try to fascinate the children, is a crime. I haven't seen a children's concert here, but I've been in a great many cities where they don't really care a damn, and the poor kids sit there in a state of catatonia with sheer ennui, praying that whoever that man is who's having a public fit on the rostrum is going to be through soon. That's a crime, because there are ways of fascinating children with music that don't have to be—by any means—on a particularly childish level. I have found that kids react very often with more interest to—let's say—Bach, than they do to Eric Coates, as I know from the case of my own child. I have an eleven-year-old daughter who's not gifted at all musically, and God knows she's exposed to enough; she's very pop-music orientated as most eleven-year-olds are—but she took instantly to the Bach Double Violin Concerto; she likes Haydn; she likes the Marriage of Figaro Overture, and when I pressed her, when I said 'Why?', she said 'Because it's so easy'. Now I don't know quite in what sense she means 'easy'—I suppose it could be in the clarity of the texture. But it's worth thinking about. We always try so desperately to do Peter and the Wolf, and transcriptions of Chopin Etudes and things for orchestra, and I have a feeling that this underrates the children terribly.

A.S.: Do you think that pop music or jazz has any value as a bridge in getting young children interested in music?

A.P.: No: the only thing is that it might lead them into the desire to play an instrument, which I am always in favour of.

A.S.: Why does pop music have such an immediate appeal to children?

A.P.: I think for any number of reasons. First of all, they're exposed to it mercilessly. I am convinced that if Webern's Pieces for Orchestra were played with the regularity that the Rolling Stones are, the kids would go off to school whistling those. I am convinced of it. And the other thing is that the attention span does not have to be long and, of course, they can dance to it. I have nothing against it: I would just like a hair more equal time.

A.S.: Their heroes are in pop music. Do you think there is a lack of heroes for young people to identify with in classical, or symphony, music?

A.P.: Yes. It's always so difficult with those adjectives. I think there aren't very many. I suppose that in America, Leonard Bernstein is a great matinee idol.

A.S.: How does that come about?

A.P.: I think maybe through television. Bernstein is first of all a great idol of mine, and I know of no American conductor I admire more. His enormous exposure on television which millions and millions of people see constantly is that which has made him a household word. Van Cliburn too. . . . It has to do most often with elements outside their real calling. In other words, no matter how brilliantly Lenny Bernstein would conduct or how brilliantly Van Cliburn would play, if it hadn't been for the mass media lending a hand they might not be great heroes; and that's where the pop stars have it all over everybody. That's really all they do—radio, television and things like that. But I'm sure there'll always be idols in both kinds of music.

A.S.: Most of the provincial orchestras do more educational music than the London orchestras. Do you think it is the place of an orchestra like the L.S.O. to do too much of this?

A.P.: Speaking in a Utopian sense, yes, I think the L.S.O. should do a lot more, because so much depends on how well the music is played the first time it is introduced to someone's mind. If it is played with a great deal of dash and expertise, it is likely to make a much greater effect than if it's played in a desultory fashion by some group

B

'I would like, if at all, to be remembered as just a good musician.'
Andre Previn with John Duffy, and
Robin McGee—basses.

that really wants to be at home at that time. Also, the thing that might make the L.S.O.—specifically the L.S.O.—a great purveyor of musical education, is the fact that the average age is considerably younger than any other I know. How old is it?

A.S.: Thirty-three.

A.P.: Thirty-three, yes. Take the Boston Symphony for instance. I think the average age has been computed to be 112. I think it is much easier for a student to identify with someone who is in the early thirties than someone who is in his late sixties.

A.S.: You have been an advocate of the open rehearsal?

A.P.: I find it is very interesting for students to find how a piece is put together initially, and perhaps more interesting than the final result. It is something they don't see very often. I also feel that there is something 'putting off' about the students putting on dark suit and white shirt, and going to sit in, what they might feel, is alien territory; whereas at rehearsal, they can come in whatever school clothes they happen to have on—I don't care what they come in—and they can sit and watch a highly professional group of people rehearsing and putting together a great complexity, and it shows them how much work it is, how intricate it can be—and that it can be great fun. I just think that the students and the kids should feel about the symphony orchestra, that they should go and see it in a very casual way. If there is nothing on at the corner cinema, then they should say 'Well, let's go to a concert' —instead of feeling that they must plan it like some great event. The more at home they feel in the environments of great music, the more they like it.

One of the difficulties is that we don't always rehearse in the place we play. We don't always know where the rehearsal is going to be, nor is there room for a great many visitors in some of the places we rehearse.

An ideal condition would be always to rehearse at the place of the concert. I can't tell what the hell things sound like in the Bishopsgate Institute—it sounds just like some sort of audible soup; it's got no relation to the balance of the Festival Hall later. I think it would make things literally ten times as easy if we really had a home. It's like if you live in hotels and you never know what hotel you're going to be in, and then suddenly you buy a house, and then you really have all your meals inside that house, and have guests over to that house. There's a kind of pride of possession and a security that goes with that, and with an orchestra of the international importance and brilliance of the L.S.O. it would be something to shoot for—to have a hall, and there to do always all our playing. But I am no acoustics expert. I am mathematically really a total idiot. I once bought a book which was highly recommended to me, called *Music is a Science* by a man called John Redfield, which is the primer on acoustics. I thought that I should not be a conductor without knowing anything about acoustics. I read the first page of that book about twenty times and then put it away and laughed a lot, because I realised that I hadn't understood one principle.

A.S.: But you have a favourite hall—not as a pianist, but as a conductor. Which halls do you like?

A.P.: Carnegie Hall in New York I think. I like the Academy of Music in Philadelphia. Of the new halls, I love the Jones Hall in Houston. The Music Centre in Los Angeles is quite good, even if it is a little over-brilliant. I have not played in a great many of the new halls in Europe. I quite like the Festival Hall—I know that some of my colleagues don't—I like it very much.

A.S.: It has a clarity, but we often feel that the strings don't really blend.

A.P.: Well, the strings do have a tendency to get a little wiry. Nevertheless, one can hear what's going on.

I frankly like wooden halls better than anything. Not only for sound but for the whole experience of sitting in them. One of the things I am particularly pleased with in the Jones Hall, which is only two years old, is that the interior is a hundred per cent wood. Even though it is a new, rather stark-looking hall from the outside, it has a great instant warmth, and the theatrical experience is wonderful. I wish halls weren't quite as severe looking—for instance, I enjoy listening to concerts at Queen Elizabeth Hall, but I can only think of the Maginot Line—and that's too bad.

A.S.: Well, you are just at the beginning of what we hope is a long association with the L.S.O. Are there any innovations which you would like to see come about during your period with the orchestra?—or is this not the time for innovation?

A.P.: Oh, I think always is the time for innovation! At the beginning of my first official season as principal conductor, I still want to feel my way a bit, not with the orchestra as much as with the city: what works and so on. I don't even know what constitutes successful concerts in terms of a draw at the moment. In going over the repertoire of the five resident orchestras for the past few years, I notice a certain trendiness at the expense of a lot of good music. I don't necessarily say that we have to do reams and reams of music that was written last Wednesday, but there's an awful lot of major musical thinking that has been left out. I don't see why every orchestra has to do the same Mahler, the same Beethoven and the same Brahms; I'd like to dredge up some music that isn't played every single week, and it doesn't necessarily have to be all that contemporary.

A.S.: You're interested in Haydn, for instance, aren't you?

A.P.: And of course, that can keep me going for ever! I'm also terribly interested in French music, which is not played much. I'm very interested in American music, which is almost not played at all, with the exception of the times we had Copland. In going over this next year's list, there is almost no Sibelius, there is almost no Mendelssohn—you know—great huge gaps.

A.S.: Are there any contemporary composers that you'd particularly like to champion?

A.P.: As you know, I feel strongly about British music. There is a great deal of it I like—it wouldn't be any trail-blazing but Britten, Walton, Tippett. The only kind of music that I seem to baulk at is the electronic music, which I do not understand, but I realise that's my loss. I don't particularly feel like worrying a lot about it at the moment, because I am much too interested in the human production of sound, before I get into the electronic production of sound. That's something to do with the fact that I go to pieces if I have to change a light bulb!

A.S.: Of course, there is performed electronic sound, as well as that laid down on tape. Do you think there is perhaps more interest where a performer is involved?

A.P.: I'm sure there is. I just simply don't take to any of it.

A.S.: How would you like to be remembered by the L.S.O. in fifty years' time? What do you want to do with us, just give good concerts or set a new style?

A.P.: No, I should like to give good concerts; I should like to resurrect certain repertoire. I've heard a lot of conductors referred to as either brilliant technicians or remarkable human beings, as masters of discipline, or precision, or whatever—I must say that I would like, if at all, to be remembered as just a good musician.

PART TWO

The Strings

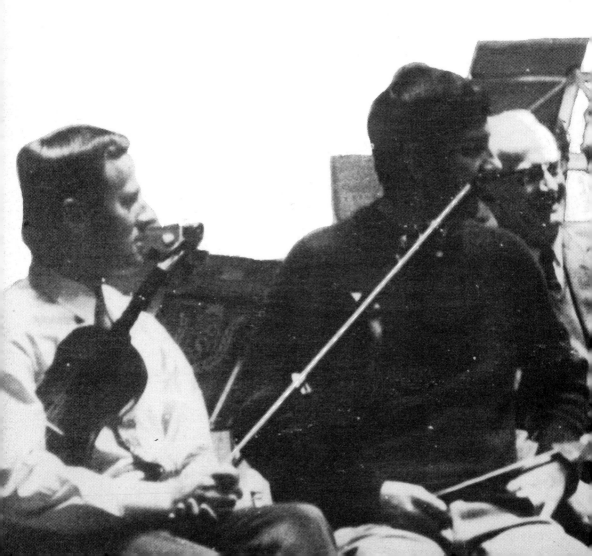

*John Georgiadis, David Measham and
John Brown. First violin section*

JOHN GEORGIADIS

Leader of the L.S.O.

The most elevated appointment among the musicians in a symphony orchestra is that of the 'leader' or 'concert-meister'. It is his lot to be diplomatic with troublesome conductors, or when a player is less than his most co-operative—a very rare occurrence—and disaster threatens, he has to be ready to pour the oil on the troubled waters.

He leads the performance too, influencing the musical style of the players, especially in the string sections.

At rehearsals he sets the bowings, in consultation with the other string principals, and makes musical remarks from time to time to all the players in all departments.

Most standard repertoire works have a set style of L.S.O. bowings and phrasings, which are only changed at the specific request of a visiting conductor, and usually altered back again after he has gone. This doesn't mean that these works receive 'standard' performances; these are just details which can be settled many ways, but on which the players have agreed or compromised as a working basis for inter-pretations that will vary infinitely from conductor to conductor.

He has to be liked by all, for he must communicate. And, of course, he must be a superb violinist, capable of exposure under the most exacting conditions.

John Georgiadis has led his young group of violinists through practically all the symphonic repertoire now.

A.S.: John, what are your priorities as leader?

J.G.: To play the violin, one; to get the A from the oboe, two; and then to be a sort of a liaison between orchestra and conductor. The in-between.

A.S.: You haven't mentioned what to most people seems to be the most important aspect of your job which is to play the solo violin parts.

J.G.: Playing a solo I would put under the first category of being able to play the violin, you see.

A.S.: So should any of the violins be able to play the solos?

J.G.: No, no, not necessarily of course, but that is the sort of prime object I suppose of sitting in the hot seat, to be able to play the notes, solos as well. I mean, when you are younger you tend to look upon that as the end—as the ultimate aim of a leader—but really it does come down to a sort of a junction between orchestra and conductor. It depends a bit on the conductor, of course; some conductors don't even want to know the leader, they prefer to be in complete control themselves.

A.S.: Do you let them?

J.G.: Oh, normally, yes, or we would have friction the whole time. There is no point in trying to rule everything, or trying to do the job exactly the same regardless of the conductor, you have got to more or less fit the circumstances, fit the conductor's personality.

A.S.: Is that attitude constantly in your mind? Do you sit there at a rehearsal feeling *responsible* for the whole orchestra?

J.G.: I can work better for a conductor when I feel I am making a useful contribution—if he takes notice of what I say or, even better still, if he asks my opinion on certain things, obviously I feel I am able to work much better than for a conductor who looks at me as though I am bonkers for even opening my mouth.

A.S.: It is important that you are a likeable person, isn't it, if he is going to cooperate with you in that?

J.G.: Oh, that is accepted of course, yes.

A.S.: Do they like you on the whole?

J.G.: I find that I am really concerned mainly that I should be liked by conductors whom I respect, and perhaps, maybe it is a slight fault on my part, but I find it very difficult even to feel any concern for conductors who are really 'no hopers'.

A.S.: What is your attitude in a situation where you regard the conductor as a 'no hoper'—you don't like him and he doesn't like you. Do you just fall back on professionalism?

J.G.: That is the ideal, really. I think George Szell summed it up very well for me when he was giving me advice on one occasion—I understand that he gives mostly disadvice, and I was receiving my portion of this, when he told me that I played behind the beat and I didn't really believe him. He did it very politely, he took me in his room and told me this, and on the box he would give me knowing winks if I was behind the beat; if I played what for me appeared to be way ahead of the beat, but for him was the right place, he gave me a little smile underneath the side of his glasses, which was a sort of an indication that I was on the right track. He told me afterwards that, for a good conductor, that is the only place you can play, right at the bottom of the beat. 'For a poor conductor', he said, 'you have got to play there regardless for the sake of the orchestra.' So when the conductor really is poor, one has to take the helm as it were at times, in a sort of discreet manner.

A.S.: Is it part of the leader's job literally to take the helm and to conduct if anything happens to the conductor?

J.G.: I would like to think it is. It always was, but it seems to have slipped by the board a bit in latter years; I have always thought that the leader should at least have the ability to make a show of it if a disaster struck and there really wasn't any alternative conductor available.

A.S.: Has it happened?   .

J.G.: Only at rehearsals; I have conducted on two occasions for Andre Previn and, earlier, before I joined the L.S.O., I did conduct three schools' concerts. Mind you, that was not at the last minute; I did have a few days in which to prepare it, and the few occasions since I have been with the L.S.O. have been small occasions when the conductor has wanted to go and listen to the orchestra from the back of the hall, or on two quite different occasions when Previn went sick. Once was with the William Walton First Symphony—I had to conduct a complete rehearsal of that. I took two and a half hours over it, to the disgust of the orchestra! The other occasion was Richard Rodney Bennett's Second Symphony, and that could have been a little bit touchy; I suggested that Richard Rodney Bennett himself do it as he was there, but he said under no circumstances would he take a baton in his hand, so. . . .

A.S.: Refreshing modesty in a composer . . . To someone not used to conducting it must be a marvellous sense of what?—to stand in front of ninety men and control the forces.

J.G.: To someone not used to conducting, it is a marvellous sense of nothing! It is bloody murder; it is absolutely blind fear for a little while wondering whether you can remember which way it goes after you have done the downbeat!

A.S.: But I remember that when you did conduct, there was a very friendly atmosphere, and if there had been any real disasters everyone would just have laughed.

J.G.: Oh, yes, I didn't feel that the orchestra held malice for me standing up there, because it wasn't that I was aspiring to the conducting position, it was that I had been saddled with it at the last minute, which is quite different.

A.S.: It is a funny thing isn't it? The orchestra has a feeling of resentment against members of its own ranks who wish to be conductors.

J.G.: Oh absolutely, yes. I think it is the same in business, where somebody who works on the same level as you suddenly makes a wild effort to get on to the next level, for instance into a white collar position; I think his mates are likely to resent those attempts.

A.S.: You have been a leader, of the London Symphony Orchestra and the Birmingham Symphony Orchestra, for seven years. So for that time you have had an unrivalled and unique opportunity to meet famous conductors, presumably talking to them socially, as well as playing for them. You see, I think being a conductor does something quite awful to a man as a human being, because of the power it gives him, just the musical power. What do you think of them as human beings in general. Have you liked them?

J.G.: Well, generally speaking, the better the conductor, the more relaxed the individual. I suppose he realises his position is secure and he is able to relax and be a human being again. The poorer conductor often raises problems of personality—this is how I have found it. Of course there are exceptions. There are still one or two of the traditional tyrants, but even so they are usually charming people behind the scenes.

A.S.: But they are going out of fashion do you think?

J.G.: Yes, it is rather a shame.

A.S.: Do you think that the fact that nearly all the orchestras in London are self-governing has anything to do with that?

J.G.: Well no, I think it is just a modern trend, you know. One looks back to Beecham and much earlier, too, for real characters on the box —more recently Sir John Barbirolli and George Szell. . . .

A.S.: Yes, but the conductors that conduct the L.S.O. must know that the impression they make on the players really determines largely whether they return?

J.G.: Yes, they can't be temperamental in the old-fashioned way; they have really got to show that they are good conductors musically and have got to be efficient, and perhaps these things would tend to hold back their natural personality.

A.S.: Which part of the job of being leader do you like most?

J.G.: I quite like playing solos, strangely enough.

A.S.: How do you approach that; it is a great responsibility suddenly to be there on your own playing solos. Does it worry you much?

J.G.: Not if I feel I've got the measure of it, you know. One or two solos can be irritating, they are so short and bitty that you have one crack and they're gone—you don't get your teeth into them.

A.S.: Do you think that temperamentally one has to be built for a job like being a leader, or is it training?

J.G.: I have come round to the belief that in most things, if you start very young, you don't have to spend your life worrying about the technicalities too much. You can therefore spend more time gaining confidence and thinking more in terms of the finer points. I had music drummed into me as a child by my father and, having started very young, I don't have to worry too much about intricacies. I mean, if I play a few notes out of tune I don't have to suddenly readjust the whole of my left hand or anything; I just get annoyed and put them right next time, as it were, in my mind. In fact it builds you up to a certain level of confidence to feel that your ability to play an instrument is not going to let you down in front of a few hundred people.

A.S.: You must have that. Did you start learning the violin very young?

J.G.: When I was six, yes. I was asked if I would like to play the violin and visualising another toy similar to football boots or a scooter, I decided, oh yes, something to show the kids; and then I was fully committed—I was locked into the bathroom to practice every day. A bathroom, of course, makes any old violin sound like a Strad!

A.S.: How much practice did you do at six?

J.G.: My father had pretty stern ideas about it; maybe half an hour or an hour every night.

A.S.: Did you have any gap when you were young? Was there a period when you gave it up?

J.G.: No, none. I really wasn't ever given the chance.

A.S.: And you were always going to be a professional violinist, were you?

J.G.: One doesn't really think anything but the fact that you are going to be the world's greatest soloist. It is in the back of everybody's mind, I think, right up until the time when reality creeps in.

A.S.: In that sense are you then in fact a frustrated soloist?

J.G.: No, because one assumes, going right the way through the Royal Academy of Music, 'I've got time yet to make it'. Whilst I was there, I found that there were many other things that went further than playing solos. I found a new interest in playing in orchestras and a new interest in chamber music and things like this; now I have really come to the conclusion that I am more suited to a varied life. I would probably never have been suited, had I had the stamina and ability, ever to have followed a solo career; I am probably more suited to the one I have now, because there are many aspects of the soloist's life that don't appeal to me in the least.

A.S.: Although you do have some of that, don't you, playing concertos?

J.G.: Oh yes, this is what I mean by a varied life. In this way, being stationed with the orchestra, I can do other things as well throughout the year, with my bread and butter as it were with the orchestra.

A.S.: Now you are married to Sue, who is a viola player, and you have three children; as well as that you seem to have a whole lot of hobbies. What other interests have you?

J.G.: I was recently given a form to fill up for the Musicians' *Who's Who*; the intriguing thing was that there was a great space for one's qualifications, which I somehow found I had to leave empty, but on the line below—there was just a single line to get it all in—it said 'Hobbies'. I found that the easiest thing to do was to put my hobbies in the qualifications zone, because there was a lot more room. At the moment, golf is playing a very large part in my life, but I do want to achieve something and it is a very difficult game. I play tennis, badminton and squash. I am very keen on model railways and I have a vast—by my standards—selection of model railways in the loft.

A.S.: Did you build them yourself?

J.G.: Well I laid it all out myself, yes. I just had to learn on the spot how to do it and I am quite pleased with the results. I also have model racing cars and sometimes we have parties with members of the orchestra and their wives and we become very unfriendly racing to very strict rules. I have always had a passion for fast cars.

A.S.: You have got two cars at the moment?

J.G.: Yes, but one is a sort of buggy-round-town as it were and the other one is our grand touring limousine.

A.S.: That is a Triumph and a Jaguar?

J.G.: Yes; I have acquired a different model Jaguar this year which is of course still a novelty.

A.S.: Does chamber music come into the hobbies?

J.G.: Oh, musical hobbies, yes. I suppose chamber music, and I have a hi-fi system which is quite good fun.

Yes, I think one can really lead quite a full life. I do govern myself now; apart from prestige work like chamber music and solos, I do an absolute minimum of outside commercial work and I really only take commercial work now if it is either phenomenally lucrative or if there is a rather poor patch with the L.S.O.

A.S.: What do you mean by commercial work?

J.G.: Well, really I am referring to film sessions, light recordings, light music sessions and jingles—music for I.T.V. commercials.

A.S.: Do you ever play any pop music?

J.G.: Yes, I have sat in bands with Cilla Black as part of the backing, and with Johnny Mathis for another.

A.S.: You don't feel that is beneath your dignity?

J.G.: Not at all—certainly not inasmuch as nearly all leaders seem to end up doing that for the rest of their life anyway. I mean you will find in those spheres of music a vast amount of talent in the string playing. You don't have to dress up in tails and get all keyed up for an afternoon or evening concert; there is no worrying about relaxing and sleeping for a couple of hours, you lead an almost 9–5 job.

A.S.: And is that what you are looking forward to?

J.G.: No, no not at all. I am quite happy as things go at the moment, taking the tension as it comes!

A.S.: If you are tense, I think you hide it phenomenally well. You are not the nervy type, anyway to a casual observer; I can see you doing this for forty years!

J.G.: I don't want to see myself working quite at this pace for forty years. There are times when it does become rather exhausting.

A.S.: Do you think that perhaps a little too much tension is put in by us because of the way symphony concerts are presented. Do we have to wear white tie and tails? Are we too formal?

J.G.: I think formality is necessary. A concert depends entirely on creating an atmosphere; that is what makes it different from listening to music on records in your own home and that is why people should go to concerts. It is because it is an occasion, an event. It is something unique. You go there and there is an atmosphere from the moment these gentlemen looking like penguins come on to the platform, sit there and then the conductor comes on. There should be an atmosphere and I think that a less formal type of dress would miss it. In fact, we find that to wear dinner jackets instead of tails usually means a concert of lesser atmosphere.

A.S.: And the playing less good?

J.G.: It is not of course necessary for it to be less good, but it is connected and it certainly has had this effect. That is why the L.S.O. stipulates tails throughout all its touring concerts.

A.S.: Is there anything about the symphony concert as it is presented now that you would like to see changed? For instance there is a whole potential audience of young people who are put off going to concerts because they feel they are a bit stuffy and formal when the music isn't necessarily stuffy or formal.

J.G.: Yes. I would say that here I suppose television could help. This is likely to get through quicker and to a much greater audience. I think it has been proved that Mr. Previn gets through to the younger audience and if these people are attracted by television one hopes that they will be drawn to concerts as time goes on. It is making the first step towards actually sitting either just behind or in front of a large orchestra thundering through some massive Tone Poem by Strauss but it is only then that you can really realise what it has to offer—the excitement of going to a live concert.

A.S.: But can the performance of a live concert with all the risks involved ever be as perfect as the reading of a recording?

J.G.: Probably not. But it is usually far more of an event. Much more of an atmosphere, providing of course that we have got the right conductor, a man who has got the orchestra into good form—fine fettle —and the orchestra is playing at its best, and then you have an event— something that happens on the spot. There might be the odd blurb or two here and there. . . .

A.S.: One of the things that we have done a lot of in recent years is touring. How do you react to this? It must be an interruption in your home life going away for several months?

J.G.: Touring is one of the attractions of the L.S.O. Many of the orchestras travel around the world these days, especially from London, and the L.S.O. certainly has its fair share of these tours; since I have been with the L.S.O. we have been right round the world once touching at places like Hong Kong.

Actually, that was quite a journey. We had a very strenuous flight in a turbo-prop plane which did it in three nine-hour hops with only hours in between before actually reaching Hong Kong; of course the nine-hour difference in Hong Kong upsets quite a lot of people—it certainly upset me; I felt permanently dizzy all week and I wanted to sleep during the day and stay awake all night. I don't really think that that particular hop helped the concerts too much.

Then we went on to Singapore and on to Australia. Such is the travelling life these days I could say that it was the second time I had been to Australia with an orchestra; I had been a few years earlier with the London Philharmonic Orchestra. We then went on—after very memorable one night stops in such magical places as Fiji, Wakiki Beach, Hawaii—to San Francisco; then we played for a week or two in New York. Since then, we have been to Florida four years running for the summer season, for about a month each time. This has been an especially nice trip as we have been able to take our families each year, and so it is not an interruption of home life.

A.S.: But this is unusual isn't it?

J.G.: Oh it is unusual and of course it is aided by the fact that we are based in one town for the four weeks, so it is not such an expensive operation to fly the family out.

A.S.: Where are the best audiences?

J.G.: In some ways, I think in London, inasmuch as they are attentive, they are quiet, and they understand the music, and silly little things like not clapping between movements—which one doesn't expect from a sophisticated capital anywhere in the world. Certainly the London audiences come out very well on this. However, I feel they are not critical enough. When a great artist perhaps isn't playing at his best—I don't feel that the audience should still nevertheless stamp their feet and bring the roof down regardless. I heard that Russian artists for instance have expressed the wish that, when they haven't played at their absolute best, the audience wouldn't still acclaim them in a fantastic manner. I recollect how in New York, when the audience found they didn't like a modern piece of music, there was no mean effort to show their disapproval—and in a way I thought, 'Well, why not? It's a positive reaction.'

A.S.: Yes, it shows more critical vitality, I suppose. I think that people don't like to show a critical attitude because they feel that it might be their ignorance.

C

J.G.: Yes, this is a very interesting phenomenon these days where critics seem loath to actually criticise anything that is ultra modern for fear of being eventually classed as condemning the avant garde—not a progressive thing to do! As a result it seems to take quite a long time before we really know, or can decide, what is actually good coming out of the new stuff, and what isn't.

A.S.: What is it like playing to an audience of children?

J.G.: I have had a lot of experience of this. In Birmingham when I was there they had a really vast schools' programme and when a thing is put forward in a really suitable manner I think it is marvellous playing to children, but I am just not convinced that it is always done right. I think programmes should never be long and they have to be highly interesting and very well explained. This is sometimes lacking a little bit. So often we find ourselves grinding through whole movements of works which really don't hold the interest of an audience of children. I think it is a little bit of a problem really to construct programmes that will hold their interest throughout.

A.S.: Is it part of an orchestra's job do you think to play to children?

J.G.: Well it has to be done by orchestras somewhere. Whether it has to be done by the London Symphony Orchestra and international class orchestras I don't know. I think probably occasionally yes, and perhaps with the use of media such as television, the best orchestras could do this to great avail.

I often think that a child will probably get more from going with its parents to a full concert—one that the parents themselves could perhaps choose wisely, because you can never get quite the same atmosphere with a children's concert in the middle of the day and in dark suits instead of tails. It is rather like a Saturday morning cinema.

A.S.: Yes, but that pre-supposes musically intelligent parents which unfortunately is not always the case even today. I think that this is one thing that Andre Previn is interested in.

Is it a good career to be an orchestral violinist?

J.G.: Yes, why not? I think so. It can wear you down and you can get tired and you can even think that you don't like music, but you are doing something that is always pleasant. You lead an interesting life, you travel, and you aren't badly paid.

A.S.: That is nice when you are young, but what about when you get older. Is it still a good job?

J.G.: I can't answer that question yet. I'll tell you in twenty-five years. . . .

A.S.: All right, then! What is your own instrument?

J.G.: Well I have now got a violin by Lorenzo Guadagnini, made in 1740.

A.S.: Is it worth a lot of money?

J.G.: Well, it cost me quite a lot of money and it has a value now of about £5,000; but it is a difficult thing to put in a book because by the time this book is printed it may be worth about £35,000!

A.S.: Are you buying it on the never-never?

J.G.: Yes, quite never-never, never-ever, so it is taking a long time. I have been playing on it now for about fifteen months and I bought it just about a year ago.

A.S.: Apart from the snob value, what makes an instrument worth all that money?

J.G.: Well, antique value mainly, of course, and competing with collectors; that's what whops the price up and also the fact that there is such a dearth of the good instruments now because so many people wish to play. And, you know, nobody is making Strads any more.

A.S.: So it is not the sound at all?

J.G.: Oh, yes, because it still seems that violins made in this period by these people are the ones with the best sound and, as I say, if only we knew *why* that was I suppose we would be making them today. It is obviously something to do with the mellowing of time and the fantastic accuracy with which they were made—the patience put into them at that time.

A.S.: But the commercial worth of the instrument is caused mainly by its antique value?

J.G.: It is demand—whether it is antique demand or players' demand. It is the actual demand for owning one and, of course, it is not a bad thing to have a good violin. I looked at it from the idea of getting on the bandwagon quick; I thought I must get a good instrument because prices seemed to be going so high so quickly.

A.S.: Now you *can* buy a violin for £20—would that be adequate for a beginner?

J.G.: Yes, provided it is set up well. I think this is so important. So often you see little rosy red violins which aren't the world's greatest things to look at but nevertheless they are serviceable instruments. But so often I am shown these things and asked what I make of them—and you really can't tell because the class of strings, the setting up of the bridge and the various points of importance are so haphazard that the violinist himself has absolutely no opportunity of showing what it can do. One must take advice on obtaining a nice set of strings; not metal if possible, some nice covered gut strings, and make sure the bridge is set up with tail pieces in the right place. That will give the violin at least a chance to do its best possible work and give the best sound it can produce.

A.S.: The leader's main responsibility is that of liaising between the orchestra and the conductor. That must be most important when there is a crisis situation: Can you remember any of these?

J.G.: Oh yes. One comes to my memory now—I hadn't been with the L.S.O. for too long.

On one occasion Mr. Rowicki was recording with us and wanted something special from a particular player and it became increasingly obvious to us that Mr. Rowicki did not feel, despite the rigid attempts at the passage concerned, that he was getting what he wanted—and what's more he felt that it was a deliberate lack of co-operation on the part of the musician. Without making a big fuss or exploding, as some conductors would have done, he put his baton down and sat there and smiled at the orchestra in a very benign fashion. Now, not fully realising what had happened for a moment, we sat there quietly, until we realised that with the smile he was implying that until something happened and this passage was put right Mr. Rowicki was going to sit there and fast for weeks—it certainly appeared like that. So, after giving it what I thought was a suitable time, I stood up and approached Mr. Rowicki and said, 'Is there something wrong?'

Mr. Rowicki then pointed out to me that he really wasn't intending to continue conducting whilst this player didn't co-operate. This then was up to someone and I was at hand and had asked the question and so it would seem to be my responsibility. I walked round to the back of the orchestra and had a few very quiet words with the musician.

A.S.: What did you say?

J.G.: I said something to the effect that, 'We know it is hard, it's tough, everybody is feeling it a bit today, but come on, it is only us you are hurting'—something to that effect. Nothing more than that.

A.S.: Did he reply?

J.G.: No. I walked back with my fingers crossed, and Mr. Rowicki then accepted my sitting down as a signal that things had been corrected. We went through the passage again which, I am very happy to say, went right, or right to the conductor's desires.

A.S.: What about the conductors who traditionally have a reputation of being very fiery: Stokowski for instance. Have you had any experience with him?

J.G.: Yes, I must say Mr. Stokowski is a real experience today. I mean here is a character *extraordinaire*. I find it hard to believe that he can really be the age that is given to him. He has incredibly blue eyes and those, linked to what, if my memory serves me correctly, is a very hooked nose, give him a somewhat sinister appearance to anybody sitting near him, especially as close as I am to him. It is always an event working with Mr. Stokowski. You will find him sitting on the podium at least an hour before the rehearsal or the recording session begins, and he will be exchanging cordialities with various members of the orchestra as they walk into the hall. Then exactly, not one second either way, exactly on the dot of three o'clock or whatever time it is scheduled to start, Mr. Stokowski claps his hand in one sweeping gesture—one big clap, and says 'Good afternoon, gentlemen, may we tune.' And the oboeist gives an A for which Mr. Stokowski usually allows 4.65 seconds and then with another sweeping clap of his hands will say, 'The Master-singers Overture', and begin on the downbeat. And of course, as just may happen, some poor inexperienced soul in the orchestra may not be prepared to play with him at that precise moment, maybe because the poor soul is still tuning his instrument or hadn't quite got the page to the right place. He doesn't quite make it to the down beat, and then Mr. Stokowski will stop and look ferociously into this person's eyes without blinking, daring his victim to look him back in the eye, and will say: 'Sir, you start when I start, and no missing a mark!'

WILLIAM BENHAM

Violin

A.S.: You are twenty-three now, Bill; have you been playing the violin for many years?

W.B.: Since I was ten; I joined the National Youth Orchestra when I was fifteen—it was a great experience and made me want to take up the violin professionally, although I knew at that time my technique was very limited. It was the first time I had played in a big orchestra and it was a great thrill—I remember we played the Brahms Fourth Symphony. I started really when I was at school at Winchester. I was very keen on rowing, actually, but I had to give it up when I started to get on with the violin because it just didn't mix. The other games like football and cricket were compulsory and I had a terrific job trying to get out of them. We had a school orchestra which was also very encouraging and then for two years, almost until I was seventeen, I played with the National Youth Orchestra. Then I met Jean Pougnet and I was very impressed by him.

A.S.: Was he impressed by you?

W.B.: Well, he was; I played the Mozart Fourth Violin Concerto and he was quite impressed. He had been a prodigy himself when he was young and in fact he kept on telling me that he had first learned this concerto when he was only eleven. At this stage he rather tried to put me off from joining the profession, for one reason or another. However, he was then running the County Youth Orchestra and he appointed me as leader; I played quite a few concertos with them.

A.S.: You say he tried to put you off joining the profession for a number of reasons—what reasons?

W.B.: Well, I think the main one was that he himself would have preferred to have gone in for engineering, but he had never had the education to do it; he told me he had always been interested in engineering and he had all sorts of gadgets around the house. He was very practical and if anything went wrong with his motorcar he would either see to it himself or take it to a garage and look underneath it. He was always interested in engines.

I went to Oxford to do engineering and I didn't like it; in fact I got in on physics, but I changed to engineering because I thought it was more practical. Unfortunately, the engineering course was not the sort of thing I was really interested in. I would really have been much more interested in art, but as it happened I had got my A levels in physics and maths, and I couldn't do anything about it. I left after the first term.

A.S.: You must have had it in your mind to be an engineer before you went to Oxford?

W.B.: No, I didn't at all; in fact I had quite an argument with my parents. I was always telling them that I would much prefer to play the violin, but then they said that now I'd got into Oxford I had better take advantage of it, and that is how they persuaded me.

A.S.: So while you were there, being miserable about this engineering course, were you playing the violin?

W.B.: Yes, I worked with quite a lot of orchestras in Oxford, quartets and things like that, but they were on the whole of a very low standard.

A.S.: So when you left Oxford it was to become a musician?

W.B.: Yes, definitely.

A.S.: And how did you set about it?

W.B.: I was already having lessons with Jean Pougnet and I thought I would just carry on and see how it worked out. He didn't think it was very advisable to go to any of the London colleges at that time because he did not have a very high regard for many of the teachers; I think he was perhaps a little prejudiced, but maybe also he was right. Anyway, I stayed with him and had lessons for two years.

Then I came across Homi Kanga when I was sent up to Newcastle to do a date with an orchestra. I had been doing casual engagements with the Worthing Municipal Orchestra: I did one season with them and one of the horn players in the orchestra put me in touch with the 'fixer' for the Newcastle date.

That's how I got there and, in fact, it was just before I was going to play a concerto that I met Homi. He said a lot of interesting things and really persuaded me to go and have some lessons from him. I arranged to get a flat in London and he began to completely revise my technique, mainly with a view to getting over the problem of intonation which is, I think, one of the greatest problems for any string player. When he thought that I was good enough, he got me a job with the orchestra of the Drury Lane Theatre and some engagements with the Bath Festival Orchestra. Then I met one or two other people, got other engagements and it all sort of snowballed. After I'd been having lessons with him for a year and a half, he sent me for an audition with the L.S.O.

A.S.: Why particularly?

W.B.: He was interested in getting me to practise more efficiently—this was one thing; he also thought it was necessary for me to acquire a more professional attitude towards music.

A.S.: And has the L.S.O. got that?

W.B.: Yes, I think it has. When I first went to a rehearsal as a member of the orchestra, I was slightly surprised at some of the jokes and the behaviour in the section, because I'd always thought that the conductor should command one's complete attention. But anyway, I soon got used to it, and I think that the jokes and the larking around—which some people disapprove of—is perhaps very good for the orchestra; some of the work we do is very repetitious and I think one has to have a bit of amusement.

A.S.: It's a sort of expression of spirit, of vitality?

W.B.: Yes, exactly. At a concert one has to play well and, if one concentrates at all the rehearsals with the same intensity, one just can't at the concert, because it isn't humanly possible. I think it's good therefore that the rehearsals should be relaxed and the concerts should be concentrated.

A.S.: I've noticed that with any conductor, even one who doesn't command respect, there is never any mucking about at a concert because the musicians somehow feel instinctively that they must be loyal to the audience and public. I've never seen a concert go to pieces because of the lack of attention of musicians. Musicians have a remarkable integrity.

And now you are one of the king-pins of the first violin section, what do you plan from here?

W.B.: Homi has plans for me to go in for the Tchaikovsky Violin Competition in Moscow next year—that is, in May or June. It requires a great deal of work, of course, so I'm taking off a few concerts. He's

—in rehearsal, violins.

not sending me because he thinks I'll win it, but because he thinks it will do me good. You hear a lot of very good players and, as long as one approaches these competitions with that attitude, I think they can be most helpful.

A.S.: You are married now?

W.B.: Yes, I met Jane in the Festival Ballet when they were in Southsea.

A.S.: Is she a musician too?

W.B.: She was actually in the wardrobe then, but she can play the violin.

A.S.: But now you're in the L.S.O. and you're married, with responsibilities and financial commitments, how is it possible for you to give up enough work to enable you to find time to practise to competition standards?

W.B.: Well, yes, you see Homi has ideas about this; he thinks that playing in the orchestra one has to be disciplined—you have to be at a certain place at a certain time, and you know that you work for three hours. In this way it's a help for organising one's own practice. I find I can't practise in the evenings if I've had two sessions. The best time to practise is in the morning, and therefore I'm trying to arrange it to get some mornings off, rather than any other time.

A.S.: Have you done any teaching yourself?

W.B.: Not really, I tried to teach Jane for a few days and gave it up.

A.S.: What's the best way to start to learn the violin?

W.B.: I think finding a good teacher is the main problem. It depends on one's own talent, of course; you've got to have somebody to be able to say whether you have any talent.

A.S.: Is it your ambition, now, at this stage, really to be a soloist rather than an orchestral player. Would you like to do both?

W.B.: I'd like to be able to play solos. I don't think I would ever become a great soloist, but I'd like to be able to play concertos now and again. I would also like to be able to play chamber music.

A.S.: Do you enjoy the musicality of playing in the orchestra?

W.B.: I do, especially at concerts. Sessions I sometimes find annoying because we have to keep stopping, rehearsing, doing the same passage about thirty times. This I find is very off-putting; it's the hard side of it. A concert is an occasion—I think I enjoy the concerts more than any other things we do.

A.S.: You don't mind being one of a team of sixteen?

W.B.: No, not at all, it's very good.

A.S.: In fact, to be a small cog in a big efficient machine is quite fun.

W.B.: Well, I think it's a very important part in a musician's training; there are so many soloists who can't play with anybody else and therefore they get so far and no further. The really great soloists can play chamber music—they can do anything.

A.S.: What about conductors?

W.B.: I think one of the oddest things is the relationship with the conductor. Orchestral players tend to be very biased against the conductor simply because they have to do what he says.

A.S.: Are you biased against him as well?

W.B.: I suppose so.

A.S.: You mean you don't like being told what to do?

W.B.: Any musician likes to have his own way of playing a piece—you have your own views.

A.S.: Yes, unless you are quite sure that the conductor knows better than you, and you respect that.

W.B.: Yes. Sometimes we have very good conductors, but we don't appreciate them always, mainly because their interpretation differs from our idea—this doesn't necessarily mean that their ideas are bad—I think everybody has their own individual idea about a piece of music.

A.S.: Organised as we are, on a more or less free-lance basis—apart from our permanent conductor, Andre Previn—we have a sort of parade of guest conductors, many of whom have only one engagement with us and then pass on. Perhaps we don't have a chance to get to know them enough musically?

W.B.: Yes, but a lot of the players in the orchestra are very good, and they all have their own ideas about how a piece should go and therefore they don't like being told somebody else's way all the time; and when you have to do it every day of the week it sometimes gets a bit much.

A.S.: Which of the conductors you have played for with us have you enjoyed most?

W.B.: I think George Szell, Colin Davis, Andre Previn, I thought these very enjoyable.

A.S.: What about Rozhdestvensky?

W.B.: Yes, very much, but I was in rather a nervous condition at that time being on the front desk. I admire him very much. Claudio Abbado I also like very much, but you can't hear what he says if you sit behind the third desk. Some people think this is a good thing, of course!

A.S.: In the first violins, which is your section, you rotate, so that you don't have a set position, do you?

W.B.: That's right. I like it very much, because some orchestras have a terrific hierarchy system—if you're at the third desk you are better players than the fourth desk and you make them know it; if you make mistakes people can be very nasty about it. But I think in the L.S.O. with this rotation system everybody is equal and it prevents any snobbishness.

A.S.: It only prevails in the first violins, the rest of the strings have set positions.

W.B.: I would have thought that the first violin section was probably more prone to that sort of thing than any other section.

A.S.: What sort of impression did you have of the orchestra as a musician coming into it—in the way it was run? Was it as you thought it would be?

W.B.: Well, I think the way it is run is absolutely excellent. One of the worst things about being a free-lance musician is having to arrange everything by telephone. With the L.S.O. you have monthly sheets, and everything is very efficiently run.

A.S.: Do you get the variety of music, though, that you would if you were free-lance?

W.B.: One doesn't get the variety of chamber music and chamber orchestras.

A.S.: What about the actual standard of instrumental playing when you first came into the orchestra?

W.B.: Well, I was quite staggered by how good it was. When I first joined the section, whoever I sat next to, I was so impressed. Now, I don't always feel the same, but this may be because I am used to it.

A.S.: In the L.S.O. we're supposed to be a democracy. Do you feel that you have enough say in the arrangements that are made for the orchestra?

W.B.: Yes, but I never seem to be wanting a say in anything, really. I'm not really terribly concerned with the arrangements that are made. I know that they'll be all right and I just accept it.

A.S.: You're mainly concerned with the playing? You haven't any interest in the administrative side?

W.B.: Not really, I feel that there are Directors there, that they know their job and that's that. I want to use the time for practising.

A.S.: Do you, nevertheless, feel a part of the L.S.O.?

W.B.: Yes, I feel that if I wanted to say something, I could, and it would be heard, so that's all right, it definitely is a democracy.

A.S.: What about things that have happened recently. What do you think, for instance, of the appointment of Andre Previn as our principal conductor?

W.B.: When the actual appointment was made I hadn't even played under him; but the first session I did was for the Lalo Symphonie Espagnole and I must say I didn't think he was all that fantastic; I wasn't terribly impressed. Then we did some television dates and I thought he was very good indeed. I liked his relaxed approach at rehearsals and the fact that he is relaxed means that one doesn't get nervous at concerts.

A.S.: He dresses in a rather modish sort of way and he has this jazz background; do you think this might draw in a new sort of audience to our concerts?

W.B.: Yes, I think so. I remember hearing that a lady, who had heard one of his television shows, wrote to the newspapers saying that this was the first time she had listened to any classical music and she enjoyed it so much, 'Thank you very much, Mr. Previn.' Obviously she only listened because it was Andre Previn, the jazz-pianist conductor.

A.S.: Just talking about the symphony orchestra more generally, do you regard it as a perfect art form or do you think it's evolving? Do you think in 50 years' time our sort of symphony orchestra will still exist, if only as a museum for nineteenth-century music?

W.B.: First, it is a perfect art form because there are so many master-pieces written for this very combination. I don't think it's evolving into anything else really, although maybe some modern composers think it is. It is a very flexible form, anyway, because the eighty players can be very different and they can do all sorts of different things. I think that it will survive because everyday life now is becoming more and more mechanical and anything that is artistic or beautiful is bound to survive.

A.S.: You play an instrument that hasn't really changed for 300 years, not in any essential detail, anyway. There are a few things, metal strings and a higher pitch, but the design of the violin is really the same.

W.B.: Actually, the worst thing about the improvement of the violin is the metal E-string. In fact we could probably do much better without it, from the point of view of tone. They say that Heifetz, when he was small, always used to use four gut strings and he used to change these strings for each concert. I don't know if that is true, but so I was told. The gut E-string doesn't last very long, only a few days; you have to keep changing it, because it goes out of tune. But then the tone of a metal E-string can be very harsh and for Mozart it certainly is much more difficult to play because of this.

Alan Loveday has a violin with gut strings which he tunes down a semitone to play unaccompanied Bach; a very beautiful soft sound and the chords are much easier to play because the strings have more give.

A.S.: Do you think you have learned anything from the players around you since you've been with us?

W.B.: Yes, I think I have.

A.S.: Has playing in a section for the last twelve months had any bad effect on your playing as a violinist?

W.B.: I don't think so; no, in fact I think I've improved while I've been in the orchestra. I have been taking lessons every ten days or so and am therefore in constant check; if anything started to slip Homi would notice it immediately and tell me so. I think it's partly because the standard of intonation in the orchestra is very high.

A.S.: Intonation is something that all the sections are working at all the time and thinking about.

We've done a series of modern music concerts with Pierre Boulez—Schoenberg, Webern and Berg mostly—did you enjoy this?

W.B.: Yes, I don't appreciate the music but I certainly admire the conducting of it. The way Mr. Boulez takes the rehearsals is most admirable.

A.S.: You don't like the music at all?

W.B.: Yes, some bits I like, but on the whole I can't really appreciate it.

A.S.: Do you dislike them?

W.B.: I think so, yes, most of them. I'm not sure what it is; it just doesn't appeal to me. I played in a small group with Andrew McGee before I joined the orchestra and we did a piece by Schoenberg called the Ode to Napoleon with a speaking voice, and I thought that was a very good piece; but it's a completely different sort of music, a completely different style. It was only four minutes long.

A.S.: Well, to please you, we'll just have to programme a lot of Beethoven and Brahms!

SAMUEL ARTIS

Second Violin

A.S.: Why do you play with a symphony orchestra, Sam?

S.A.: I play with the symphony orchestra mainly because I enjoy it—I enjoy the music, and the people I work with.

A.S.: Quite a few things pay more money than a symphony orchestra. Is it mainly a question of the repertoire, or companionship?

S.A.: The companionship comes into it quite a bit; I think that I would like the menu to be changed slightly, with a little bit of something in baroque style on the menu, from time to time.

A.S.: The L.S.O. does sometimes play baroque music, and old music, but not enough for you?

S.A.: No, because we play with a symphonic style. I don't think we do it often enough. I don't think it's an economic proposition for a symphony orchestra to keep cutting down. It means that half the orchestra's unemployed.

A.S.: So you arrange to play in small orchestras as well as the L.S.O.? Most people would think being in the symphony orchestra is a full time job.

S.A.: A chap can get off, he can get off to work elsewhere and for practice. The L.S.O. is still the best orchestra in this country. It has been for quite a time.

A.S.: We do a lot of concerts for children at the Royal Festival Hall—what do you think of the quality of those?

S.A.: If you're doing this sort of thing, if there's no previous build up, the programme must be very carefully chosen; the tendency is to be too heavyweight for youngsters. The ages vary so tremendously and its ridiculous to believe that such varied ages can all listen to the same programme. A lot of them sit there quite bored, though one or two get quite a lot from it, of course.

A.S.: But you might also say that if they are being exposed to music that they are not understanding or enjoying at that moment, at least they are in contact with it. Do you think on balance that it does harm?

S.A.: At best it's a waste of time. If you've got them there for an hour and a half just think what you can do. I don't think it's good enough to let it rub off on them. You've got to delight them, to help them to enjoy music, and you've got to excite them; there's so much music in our repertoire to excite: say, the Corsair Overture, which must do something to any human being wi h feet to tap; I don't know who chooses the programme—I can't think it's the orchestra. I think probably the conductor has most to do with it.

I think in this case they are a little bit out of touch, and one has got to move amongst children to see what they want. They do want a lot of pop, and the reason they want pop is because it does something to your toes, and it's good to feel excited about anything, and if you want to bounce up and down and jump up and down I think it's a good thing —it's a stimulus. And when they come to our concerts they should feel this too, because classical music can do this—you can dance to it.

A.S.: You've been with the orchestra for fourteen years Sam, it must have been a very different orchestra when first you joined. Who was the leader then, was it Hugh McGuire?

S.A.: Yes, it was Hughie, although when I first played in this orchestra it was George Stratton, in 1947.

A.S.: Was the orchestra as busy in those days, as it seems to be now?

S.A.: Not quite so busy. We used to spend more time travelling about—doing lots of out-of-town concerts. We used to go up to Ipswich, and we had the Three Choirs Festival. I think more time was spent in travel, so although it's true to say we weren't so busy actually working, our time was taken up as an orchestra probably almost as much as it is today.

A.S.: Now we do less travelling and less out-of-town concerts. This is a pity in a way, isn't it?

S.A.: It's a good thing to take music abroad, to take music to the provinces and around the countryside. On the other hand, one does get tired of sitting in a car, especially in the middle of February when snow is just up above the windscreen wipers.

A.S.: Looking at it in the context of music nationally, I think it is a great pity that music is so centralised in London—a pity for music, a pity for the people who don't come to London, and also, just looking at it selfishly, a pity for us. I would have liked to have had a few years playing in a provincial orchestra, were the financial return reasonably comparable with London, but of course there is such a big difference between what you can earn in London and in the provinces, isn't there? The standards too are very different.

S.A.: A lot of people would prefer to be in their own neck of the woods as it were—I'd be quite interested to live in Yorkshire, which is where I was bred.

Since I have been playing with the orchestra I have been twice round the world, once in each direction. I think Japan was fascinating; the people were so different. As far as I could see they were very, very courteous, always ready to smile, especially the children.

A.S.: And they were so interested in Western music.

S.A.: I think they comprised some of the best audiences we have ever played to. It didn't matter where you went, there was tremendous enthusiasm, especially in Shizuoaka.

A.S.: The town they call the 'Vienna of Japan', isn't it?

S.A.: We had a very marvellous reception there. I think the kids on the platforms—do you remember the little band with those kids playing on harmonicas, guitars, various wind instruments? There were about thirty youngsters and some real rousing overtures—and there was no music, they were all playing from memory. Very, very efficient. I suppose this is what we liked about Japan—they are terribly efficient. From the Tokyo Express right down to the building of concert halls.

A.S.: There were some superb concert halls, new ones too, which seemed to me, all of them, to have a warm resonance, that was nice to play in, and yet they had the clarity as well.

S.A.: They've done a lot with concert halls that we haven't been able to do over here. I don't think people here know too much about what makes a good sound, about acoustics.

A.S.: Last night when we were playing the Berlioz Mass in the Albert Hall, which had just been fitted with these flying saucers in the roof, I thought they had cured the echo and yet not spoiled the warmth of the sound.

S.A.: Well, I think it's very difficult to tell from the platform. I've heard it said by several in the audience that there is a difference, but I think one would have to have a pretty exhaustive number of concerts to really test it out.

A.S.: There is one thing you hear all the time when you talk to musicians, and that is about the lack of real support—which comes down eventually to money, I think.

S.A.: And it comes down to business, because basically we're a nation of shopkeepers.

A.S.: But then people will say, is there any real reason why subsidies should be on a high level, when the arts are not appreciated by the masses—the sort of masses who would provide five hundred thousand pounds a year for one orchestra as in Berlin? Is there any reason why people should support a subsidy at this level here?

S.A.: This is a vicious circle; if the thing is available, people will obviously grow to love it as long as the quality is right.

A.S.: It's something, then, that should be stepped up by degrees?

S.A.: I should think so.

A.S.: And always a little ahead of public opinion.

D

S.A.: Yes, it must be; you must give a lead and it must come from the top.

A.S.: Just recently the appointment of Andre Previn as principal conductor was announced. What's your view of this appointment?

S.A.: Well, you're thrusting the microphone straight at me! I think he's a very pleasing personality; I think he probably realises that he's got things to learn about the art of conducting, and the art of dealing with an orchestra. At least he's got vitality; he can produce music, when he's happy with the music: for instance, Rachmaninov and Vaughan Williams—he enjoys this sort of music. I think other music exposes him somewhat; he seems not too much at home and this rubs off on to the orchestra. But I am sure that with experience on both sides we shall probably come a little closer to what is required. I remember when Furtwängler came to the L.P.O. many years ago, nobody could follow his beat and it took at least six months to settle down; I think Andre Previn is something like this. I think this is possibly my big criticism of him at the moment. I don't know whether this is for general publication, but I would love to say this to Andre himself, and I probably will as soon as I. . . .

A.S.: You may have to!

S.A.: But I'm sure, knowing his personality, that he would welcome straightforward criticism, if it's constructive and well-meant.

A.S.: What's your view of the approach of Andre Previn to the public; it's essentially a young approach; his aim is to appeal to a new young audience. Do you think he's going about this in the correct way?

S.A.: Well, I've been here fourteen years, and I'm a little sceptical. But then I've sort of grown comfy in the orchestra, and its image is changing, and, because I've been here fourteen years, it's a little difficult for me to change so abruptly; I am a little sceptical about it. He's a younger man—but, damn it he's not! He just looks younger, perhaps. But I'm not even sure about that. I think it's a good thing that one does try to appeal to a younger audience, but I hope that in appealing to a younger audience we're not going to lose our more mature audience. I think one shouldn't worry too much about appealing to a particular type of audience. What one has got to do is to put on stimulating, exciting music, and you'll get them all!

ALEXANDER TAYLOR
Principal Viola

A.S.: You were with the London Philharmonic for eleven years and you have only been with us just over a couple of months now, so you have not had much time to look round the L.S.O. really, but have you been able to draw any comparisons between the two orchestras?

A.T.: Yes, I think the biggest difference to me is between the first fiddle sections. I think the unanimity, the brilliance and style of the first fiddle section here is very remarkable. Perhaps also the wind solos are more noticeable, more defined.

A.S.: What about the atmosphere in our orchestra—do you think it is a happy one?

A.T.: Oh, I think it is. It seems a lot more informal; very distinguished people, like Copland, who come along to conduct are treated less like gods than in the London Philharmonic. When these very distinguished boys came along to the Philharmonic, everybody sat there very hushed—whereas here the chaps say: 'Oh well, let's get on with it.'

A.S.: Most viola players have started as violinists, haven't they—were you a violinist to start with?

A.T.: I was, but I just felt that I preferred the viola. My father used to play both instruments, so both instruments were at hand—and I found myself preferring the viola on sound and everything about it, particularly the bottom ranges; this has always interested me more than top register. To me a great attraction is the darker colour of the viola—and the Brescian instruments have a particularly dark colour which is rather important in a modern string band because there is a tremendous difference between the actual compass of the viola and the cello.

A.S.: Do you regard the viola as what Lionel Tertis called it 'the Cinderella of the orchestra'?

A.T.: Not nowadays; I think that is past—mainly because of Tertis's own efforts. He was really a colossal artist.

A.S.: Yes. He wrote to us after a recent performance of Ein Heldenleben and I replied to the letter; I mentioned that we were doing this book and I pointed out that most of the books about a symphony orchestra seemed to have been put together by viola players, including his own *Cinderella No More,* which is really his autobiography.

Do you have much time for anything else apart from playing the viola? As principal viola of the L.S.O. you are obviously very much in demand for every engagement—do you have much time?

A.T.: Yes, I try to make use of it but far too often I find myself sitting at home with a newspaper in my hand when I know I should be doing something else. I have done a fair amount of research into the repertoire for the viola as a sort of sparetime interest.

A.S.: Have you come up with any surprises?

A.T.: There are some marvellous classical pieces. This was, of course, the biggest hole in the repertoire—eighteenth and early nine-teenth century pieces.

A.S.: I know there is a wonderful Telemann viola concerto; is there much else?

A.T.: There is a fair amount from that time, or from just a little bit later. The Stamitz family did a tremendous amount; there are about a dozen concertos all by the Stamitz family. Then there are one or two Beethoven pieces, Schumann, Glazunov, some Bach obbligatos in the cantatas—various bits and pieces like that. But it takes time; the ideal thing is to visit all the main European capitals, get into the libraries and museums, and really get down to the catalogues there and look amongst the stuff that isn't catalogued.

A.S.: Are you allowed to examine original manuscripts and copy them?

A.T.: In certain cases, yes, but most places now have a very good microfilm service and you can have things filmed. The library of the Friends of Music in Vienna is marvellous for that. There are lots of eighteenth century sonatas in the collection there and they have a very good microfilm service.

A.S.: Do you edit the parts and prepare them for publication?

A.T.: I try to leave them as near to the original as possible, but there are some mistakes obviously in first editions, terrible misprints and so on. I haven't really submitted any for publication for the terribly selfish reason that I want to get something out of them myself.

A.S.: You perform them?

A.T.: I would like to, yes, at some stage or other. I have recorded a couple of sonatas—they are very nice sonatas indeed, by a man called Francesco Trevanni.

A.S.: So you obviously enjoy playing solos, concertos and sonatas —isn't it a bit frustrating to be in the viola section, in the middle of the chord all the time?

A.T.: It depends on the programme; you have some programmes where the viola parts aren't particularly interesting, but by and large there is a fair bit of interest in most of them. In a way, you can enjoy what is happening in other parts, in Haydn particularly. There is a great deal of interest—Mozart is usually interesting for the viola, but the Beethoven symphonies are not—I personally do not find them as interesting as many of the Mozart parts. The English composers have made a big contribution to the interest of the viola section in music of the early twentieth century—Elgar and Vaughan Williams and people like that; there are really lovely viola parts in some of their music.

A.S.: What sort of problems does one have as a section leader in an orchestra? In the violas you have got twelve very different personalities and sometimes there must be difficulties.

A.T.: In the first place the question of the person you are sitting with in a section—it doesn't matter what desk you are at—is a matter of luck and afterwards a compromise approach; it is very difficult for a principal to make any sort of concessions to personal differences, because if he does so he might find that very soon people are all sitting at individual stands.

A.S.: On what sort of basis is the seating of a section—any string section—worked out; is it on merit, are the best players always at the front, or what?

A.T.: No. I think it is a mixture of things, a mixture of merit, age and experience.

A.S.: So where do you put merit, age and experience, in the front or at the back?

A.T.: What I would place is principally a sound, taking it for granted that beyond a certain standard a person will read reasonably and accurately and be a good ensemble player; what I want is particularly the sound, because this is one of the things that can deteriorate if an orchestra is particularly busy and it is the thing that you have to nurse a bit.

A.S.: Particularly if you are not heard—if you are just playing in a section?

A.T.: Yes, for everybody from the very front to the very back, you have to nurse the sound a bit in any professional symphony orchestra.

A.S.: Does a professional player in an orchestra have to do much practising—private practice?

A.T.: I would say he has to do a certain amount. It depends really whether he is content to play at a certain level or move on—it does vary a great deal and different people have a different approach to this sort of thing.

A.S.: What is your approach?

A.T.: I like to do a few basic things—perhaps just half an hour if

I have got some sort of social arrangements, or the odd morning. The things that can go seem to be intonation, vibrato and control of very soft and very loud playing—these are things that one can let slip very easily.

A.S.: Do you regard yourself as being at the top of your profession now or do you have other ambitions?

A.T.: I would like about three months' notice on that question!

A.S.: Are you doing now what you wanted to do as a student?

A.T.: No. I think as a student you have all sorts of notions which have very little relation to what people have to do when they leave the institution. You don't really realise how competitive this profession is or how very peculiar it is insofar as human relationships are concerned. The remuneration bears very little relation to the actual value of the work, musically speaking. In many ways it is a topsy-turvy profession.

A.S.: What is your favourite musical activity currently?

A.T.: Well, I am a new member of the L.S.O. and I am very enthusiastic about the work that they do.

A.S.: Do you prefer concerts or recording?

A.T.: I prefer recordings; I make no bones about that. I find that the finished product is much more satisfying. A concert performance that comes anywhere near a fine recording is very few and far between.

A.S.: But doesn't a performance at a live concert have more atmosphere and spontaneity?

A.T.: I must be quite honest about this; it is a lot more exacting from a physical point of view than actually doing recordings with the orchestra. I think you can detach yourself a little bit more and I think there is a greater attention to detail.

A.S.: But don't you get involved in the drama of a concert?

A.T.: Yes. I find that very satisfying; I may perhaps have rather a selfish attitude but I find that concerts are much more tiring and, to make a comparison between the L.S.O. and the L.P.O., my London Philharmonic series was much more tiring for this very reason. Although I was sitting in a lower position there were many more concert performances and a completely different kind of schedule. The London Symphony Orchestra does much more recording.

A.S.: You see, I think that the reason for being a symphony orchestra is to give symphony concerts. I think the recording side may be more lucrative, but it is really a sideline; orchestras exist to perform for people.

A.T.: But I think they might in fact have a much wider listening public if they spent more time in recording studios. I think here they give satisfaction to a wider range of public and I just think the whole business of recording is much more satisfying.

A.S.: Well, is it a healthy musical trend? There is a whole generation of young people, who listen to pop and light music, but who associate the noise of a violin section with something that comes out of a loud-speaker that you switch on and not with people sitting there and actually playing at all. Isn't that unhealthy?

A.T.: I think in many ways it is, but I think the whole business of concert-giving is something that could be vastly improved on. A lot of the concert halls built nowadays—anywhere, not just in this country—have acoustics that leave a very great deal to be desired. The Festival Hall to my mind is very unfair to instruments of the middle register in particular, because of the lack of resonance.

A.S.: What sort of hall do you like to play in?

A.T.: My own favourite hall is the one at Stuttgart; it is a very modern hall with a crescent-shaped balcony. I thought it was very good—very fair to all departments.

A.S.: What about chamber music—you haven't mentioned that.

A.T.: I would have liked to have done a lot more than I have, it is just that it hasn't come my way and I haven't sought after it.

A.S.: Many people think of the string quartet as the natural home of a viola player. Do you feel that you have missed the boat?

A.T.: I think that is pretty fair; I think I have as far as that is concerned. But there again, a string quartet player in a quartet that reaches the best standard spends a tremendous amount of time away from home—and I am too fond of my home life for that.

A.S.: What are the duties of the principal viola?

A.T.: In the first place to fit in with the rest of the orchestra, to see that the bowing is arranged so that it runs parallel with the fiddles.

A.S.: Is that just for appearance or has it any musical validity?

A.T.: It has a lot of musical validity, especially as far as phrasing is concerned; if you have got two different kinds of sound coming out, this is a definite fault. There are times when the fiddle bowing doesn't suit the viola, particularly in the case of fast bowing strokes; if you try to keep the strokes identical, the viola strings won't speak because of the thicknesses of the viola strings. But in general you can say that they have to be the same. And, of course, as well as that, the principal has to deal with matters of ensemble and balance.

A.S.: You were with the London Philharmonic Orchestra for eleven years; do you think that you are going to stay eleven years with the London Symphony Orchestra?

A.T.: Well, it depends on many things; whether I am satisfied with them, whether they are satisfied with me.

A.S.: What are the signs at the moment?

A.T.: All I can say is that I am very happy.

A moment of concentration for Patrick Hooley and Alan Smyth, violas.

DOUGLAS CUMMINGS

Principal Cello

A.S.: Do you enjoy playing with a big symphony orchestra—up to now you have played mostly with the smaller groups, haven't you?

D.C.: I enjoy it immensely. It was brought most home to me today when we were playing a Mozart Piano Concerto with Andre Previn. He has great style, to play Gershwin and then Mozart, and to play them both equally well is most remarkable. He was conducting at the same time, and it was really quite something. Soon after I arrived we did the Mahler Resurrection Symphony and, never having heard it played before in a symphony orchestra of any quality, to suddenly be in the centre of such a wonderful sound, and such a wonderful work, was to me a fulfilment of a dream.

A.S.: What sort of playing had you done?

D.C.: Mainly chamber orchestras; it is entirely different.

A.S.: Do you mean that you have to play louder in a symphony orchestra, or softer and more delicately, or more sensitively—what is the difference?

D.C.: In a chamber orchestra the one person is in a way even more important; on the other hand of course it is all soft playing. In a symphony orchestra, you have to really play and the works are generally, with very few exceptions, much more difficult.

A.S.: You had only been with the L.S.O. a couple of months when you were required to play the cello solo in the slow movement of Brahms' Second Piano Concerto with no less a pianist than Claudio Arrau. You must have found this a terrifying experience, or did you enjoy it?

D.C.: It was a terrifying experience—an experience of a lifetime to sit in a concert hall opposite Arrau. It is perhaps the most sublime piano concerto and the cello is unduly honoured because the main theme in the Slow Movement the piano doesn't have. But playing with Mr. Arrau was entirely simple; he is such a great artist. He played the music—he is a most inspired man—and I felt tremendous on that occasion because he was passing the inspiration through to me. On other occasions when I have played the solo it has been much more difficult because I have had to create the music. With Arrau I just played and the music came out.

A.S.: Since then you have played concertos outside the L.S.O. You have something planned with us now, haven't you?

D.C.: I hope to play Andre Previn's Cello Concerto in October. It's a very good piece. Andre is a very good writer indeed. It's marvellous to me to be able to play a piece in collaboration with a composer. Piatigorsky—whom I studied with in California—once wrote to Walton and asked him to write a concerto which he did in close collaboration with Piatigorsky; the two working together produced a great work. The opportunity for me to be able to play Previn's piece and work with him on it is a very great honour.

A.S.: You play the Dvorak and Elgar concertos?

D.C.: The Elgar is a great work; I've only played it once. The Dvorak I've played several times; it's a magnificent work to play. The Schumann, of all concertos, I love playing most of all; it's the most lyrical of concertos. The classical ones are perhaps the most difficult...

A.S.: In the orchestra, what are your musical likes?

D.C.: Since joining the orchestra I've gone through phases. I played a lot of Berlioz at first—in a way I had a major affair with him. I read his memoirs and absolutely fell in love with them and looked forward to playing all his music because it was virtually all new to me at the time. I have a gramophone at home and I spent all my time annoying everyone around me playing his music non-stop, full blast day and night.

A.S.: And it is a very full blast, isn't it?

D.C.: I'm very much a romantic type. Mahler's works I enjoy immensely.

A.S.: Is it a regular habit of yours, to read about a composer when you are playing his works in the orchestra—is it a process of self-education, or a way of enjoying his music more? Or did that only happen with Berlioz?

D.C.: I read a little about Mahler when we recorded the First Symphony with Horenstein. I enjoy reading a little about composers, but this is on a superficial level—my concern is not with techniques of composition, I am more interested in certain aspects of their lives.

A.S.: Although you have been with us only a short time, you have played quite a lot of music. Who is your favourite composer?

D.C.: I think, without any question of doubt, Mozart. To me he was entirely a natural genius. He obviously wrote exactly what came into his mind and as he felt, he created; he could create anything. I think that he involves one whilst one is playing; playing Mozart one feels more that one is an intimate part of the music.

A.S.: Like Mozart, your father is a viola player, and is well known as a teacher?

D.C.: He was born in Australia and came over here in 1933. He always has taught and he has helped me a terrific amount. My brother is seven years older than I am. He is a violinist in the L.S.O. and we get on very well together—I hope he would agree with me. My sister, who is married to an Italian viola player, is probably the most gifted of the three of us: she's a very fine violinist. The funny thing is that we had a quartet in the family, but we have never played together.

A.S.: Do you like the way the L.S.O. is organised—the self-governing system? Do you ever wish that we had a more autocratic set-up? Do you ever wish that there was one man that you could go to and blame when things didn't go right?

D.C.: Well, there are nine people on the committee—I usually go to one of them when I have a moan, which unfortunately is quite often.

A.S.: Was there any resentment against your L.S.O. appointment, because you are so young and, I suppose, by definition you are inexperienced? I know there are a lot of very experienced older players around you. Did they welcome you?

D.C.: Absolutely a hundred per cent. They were terrific to me and had no resentment, which was very nice for me. When you get people who are entirely behind one man, and want to play, and are allowed to play, and not be repressed at all, you get the kind of atmosphere I hope to create in the cellos.

A.S.: Do you have enough free time away from music, do you think?

D.C.: Of course it is difficult. What I dislike are the nine-hour days, because that means that one is going the whole day and one doesn't have a chance to breathe at all.

A.S.: Well, what can be done about that? The reason for it all is the financial climate and the lack of subsidy and so on. We have to achieve an income of half a million a year now from performances in order to pay our own fees and administrative costs.

If you are a principal cello in London doing many nine-hour days, do you have enough time for girl friends?

D.C.: Yes. The one wonderful thing about this orchestra is that it has a certain atmosphere which seems to be conducive to young ladies. For some reason it seems to be a great honour for them to go out with gentlemen from the London Symphony Orchestra, and I must say that since joining the orchestra I have needed less time for young ladies, and I have had much greater success. But I daren't say any more!

A.S.: What do you think about the L.S.O. not having any women members?

D.C.: That is its best point, I think, because I played in a chamber orchestra that had women members. For some reason women players

'Firstly music, secondly eating—that for me is living.'
Douglas Cummings, cello. ▶

become very hard in one way or another. I don't think it is worthwhile having them in.

A.S.: Aren't they as good as men?

D.C.: Generally, no; of course, there are exceptions.

A.S.: Your sister, for instance?

D.C.: My sister, yes. There are exceptions. I am afraid that I am very old-fashioned. I think a woman's main role in life is different from a man's, and I don't think that any amount of work on their part will ever change that basic fact.

A.S.: As a member of the younger generation of musicians, what do you think of the younger generation of concert goers? Do you think they are more intelligent than people were a few years ago, or less so?

D.C.: The London Symphony is quite remarkable in its audience because, first of all, they do not go to concerts for any snob reasons. In London the audiences are very good. They are very polite always, but I think they generally know what is good.

A.S.: Apart from music and girl friends, what other interests have you got?

D.C.: I am afraid my other interests are virtually non-existent. I wish to explain that I am very very lazy; I enjoy eating very much, which is rather obvious if you look at me; and I enjoy travelling and seeing things. Before I joined the L.S.O. I used to have two or three odd days off and then I would go to Paris—I actually lived there for a year—and I would walk around the parks, read, go out and have marvellous meals all on my own, and thoroughly enjoy myself. I just enjoy doing that at the moment. But remember I am still studying in a way—I still regard myself as a student. I am lazy, though; I have this thing to fight against. I very rarely feel like practising.

I enjoy driving immensely, but I am too lazy really to find out about cars. What I should love to do is learn to fly or glide, if I ever had the time. I am afraid that in the matter of interests I am very dull, because the things that most occupy my mind are firstly music, secondly eating—and I don't mean just eating in quantity. When I was travelling with the London Mozart Players, I used to take *The Good Food Guide* with me and I would find out some small place in the country run by charming people, and have a fabulous meal at the end of it. It sounds as if I just like enormous quantity, but I really simply like impeccable cooking. That I enjoy doing most of all in nice company —it doesn't matter who the company is—and that for me is living.

A.S.: Pretty basic creature comforts apart from your music then?

D.C.: I am afraid so, yes!

JACK LONG

Cello

A.S.: You have been with the London Symphony Orchestra for about twelve years and before that you were in other London orchestras?

J.L.: Yes, I was with the London Philharmonic Orchestra in the late 1950s and I came here as sub-principal cello in 1958. I started my career at the age of fourteen at 'Joe Lyons', which was the best experience a young player could have. There was a tremendous amount of sight-reading and, during the breaks between pieces, I would have my studies up on the stand.

A.S.: What sort of living did you make?

J.L.: £5 a week—I had three or four years like that.

A.S.: Was the Musicians' Union at all strong in those days?

J.L.: Well, those *were* the Union rates! Theatre people were getting £2 10s. a week. In those days if you did a gramophone session— the old 78s—it was worth about ten bob. There aren't the same opportunities today; the theatres, the cinemas, the restaurants where a young player could gain sight-reading experience. If he is talented, he is thrown straight into a symphony orchestra. I think the technical standard today is higher, but sometimes at the expense of sound.

I think some of the professors at the colleges of music don't analyse their pupils sufficiently. They should really do this pretty quickly at the start of the course; they should say to their pupil: 'Well, look here, you are going to enter the orchestra sphere and I think it would be a good idea if you knew some of the repertoire.' Some of these old institutions, good as they may be, have professors who have never played in an orchestra and therefore don't know the repertoire.

A.S.: Some of the musical institutions take as their premise the fact that they are primarily designed to produce solo artists.

J.L.: Well, this is ridiculous! When you come to technique, you have got to use your intelligence—you have to think very carefully about how you practise; you can practise on completely the wrong lines. For instance, there are a lot of exercises which, if they are not applied in the correct way, can make you musclebound—you know this yourself.

A.S.: How old were you when you first met the cello?

J.L.: I was about six, I suppose. My family were musical in an

amateur way. My father bought a cigar box and a broom handle, made a bridge, put a metal string on it and marked out all the notes from the top near the bridge all the way down. I used to play things like Rock of Ages and Abide with Me.

A.S.: So when did you progress to a proper cello?

J.L.: When I was about eight years old I got a cello. It was one that we bought from Wilton Church after my father had contributed a small sum to the offertory and it turned out to be a fine old English cello by Thomas Kennedy.

A.S.: You had an opportunity to go to the Royal Academy of Music?

J.L.: Yes, I passed for the Ada Lewis Scholarship, but I didn't take it up because I had a very tempting offer to go to South Africa as a professional player. The cellist who had gone out there before—I won't mention his name—got DTs on the boat. I had three jobs—I used to play on the radio, I used to play in a cafe during the daytime, back to the radio station from 6 to 7, and from 7.30 onwards at a famous cinema, so I was earning £17 a week at the age of 17 and I was paid it all in gold sovereigns.

A.S.: How long were you in South Africa?

J.L.: Four years—and after that I wanted to return to England but I had no money, I had spent every ha'penny.

A.S.: What had happened to all the sovereigns?

J.L.: I had spent them in the most reckless way imaginable; I had sown all my wild oats and more besides, but I thoroughly enjoyed every moment of it and looking back now I have no regrets whatsoever.

A.S.: And what do you say about the cello as a career. A musician's life is precarious, of course.

J.L.: No—this word precarious was used by my parents when I said I wanted to be a professional. Well, touch wood, I have never been out of work except during the slump—which wasn't my fault—in the 1930s. Any occupation is precarious. If you are selling shirts in a shop and you don't sell enough—well, the manager will tell you that you are not good enough as a salesman and you are out. If you don't do your job properly, then your occupation is precarious. Anything you do in life has got to be done thoroughly and to the very best of your ability. People say that as you get older, the less inclined you are to work. I think this is rubbish—the older you get, the harder you work, because you have competition coming up from behind. The other day, Casals said to Piatigorsky, who very seldom appears in public: 'You are a

◀ *'No regrets whatsoever'.*
Jack Long and Martin Robinson, cellos.

E

young man'—he is seventy and Casals is ninety-three—'and you are not playing in public enough; well, it's time you bucked your ideas up.' Now this is the sort of spirit you want!

A.S.: Now what for you, Jack, has been the chief reward of having been a musician and a cellist for all these years? What would you say are the prizes?

J.L.: There are so many prizes; being able to travel and see the world at other people's expense, and knowing conductors, concert halls and situations that otherwise one would not have known. You may get a sort of sense of occasion out of younger conductors, but for me, I always have to remember past performances, for instance Beethoven's Pastoral Symphony with Kleiber—I will always remember that. When the performance finished some of the players were already off the platform, but I sat there absolutely transfixed.

But mainly the reward is being a competent musician and trying to fulfil every atom of your talent. I am still as enthusiastic about this profession, and about music, as I was when I first started.

MARTIN ROBINSON
Cello

A.S.: Martin, you joined the London Symphony Orchestra quite recently, about 2½ years ago; what had you done before that?

M.R.: I'd been principal cello at Sadlers Wells, played with the Covent Garden Orchestra and had two summer seasons with Max Jaffa at Scarborough, all good experience. The trouble with the system now is that you get thrown in at the deep end. After three or four years at the Academy, you are expected to go out and get a job; and a lot of the colleges, because their students rely on grants from the education authorities, tend to concentrate too much on producing teachers. People who are potentially good players have to spend too much time taking teaching diplomas when they should be practising or at least playing their instruments. Their playing suffers because they haven't time to do enough practice.

A.S.: If you get a job playing in an orchestra, like the one at Scarborough for example, what sort of standard is expected?

M.R.: Quite a high standard—at Scarborough there is a tradition and a whole library of music that dates back for heaven knows how long; Holst used to play the trombone there. Actually, to be honest, all the people I knew at the Academy, if they were good enough, did get straight into a big orchestra. Not perhaps the wind players, because there are a lot less opportunities for wind players to go straight into the profession.

A.S.: How old were you when you first started to learn the cello?

M.R.: I was just eleven. I began at the Manchester College with Oliver Vella, and later with Christopher Gough. When I first started I had a lot of trouble with my technique. I tried to make the loudest, sexiest noise I possibly could, and when I had to play fast, it was impossible—I got musclebound.

A.S.: What made you join a symphony orchestra rather than any other kind of group?

M.R.: I wanted to play in a string quartet—most string players would really like to do that. It's the pipedream that most people have. I was in a good quartet at the Manchester College of Music; we had the chance to go to a university as resident quartet, but the first violinist wanted to get married. We had only been offered about £15 or £16 a week and he said that he couldn't possibly afford it, so the whole idea fell through and the quartet came to rather a sad end. So I came to London and starved for a while. Then I heard that there was a vacancy in the L.S.O., so I wrote and came along and did an audition at the Royal Festival Hall.

The audition was in a room where all four walls had mirrors and when I was sitting there playing, and there were people looking at me, I could see them in these mirrors and it looked as if there were about ninety people all staring at me. It was a bit of a nightmare and I was very scared. The L.S.O. sent me a nice letter saying: 'We like your playing, but we don't think you are experienced enough—come back again in a year.' So I went away and played as principal cello at Sadlers Wells Opera and with the Philomusica of London. When the year was up, I came back to the L.S.O. and did another audition; this time they let me in and here I have been ever since.

A.S.: Playing in a symphony orchestra, you are only one of—usually —ten cellos, aren't you? Is that as interesting as being the only one, or one out of two or three?

M.R.: The main thing I have been curious about was to find out how other people play, what standard they had reached and how far I still had to go. The first time I played with the L.S.O. I went to Kingsway Hall where they were recording one of the Dvorak symphonies and they put me next to Peter Muscant, who had always been to me a sort of legend. I remember the first thing he said to me:

'If you're not sure what's happening, keep quiet, so that you don't mess it up.' I kept very quiet for those first three hours; I was so scared it wasn't true.

For the first six months, I thought that every one of the other nine cellists was a genius. They used to rattle through all the standard repertoire and I would just be groping around. I would see these pieces before the rehearsal and everybody would be sitting there, very calm and collected; when they played they seemed to be whizzing all over the instrument and looking very competent.

A.S.: And don't you feel that about them now?

M.R.: Not quite as much—you gradually discover how people can play; you listen to the people around you and gradually you get more confident. Now I find the most interesting part of the whole business is picking other people's brains—finding out how different people play different things; the little technical tricks that people have for getting round various passages.

A.S.: And did you discover any little trick of your own to help you when you were really feeling scared?

M.R.: The only trick that really works is to take the parts home and practise them and then you feel that you can really play them.

STUART KNUSSEN

Principal Double Bass

A.S.: Would you like to say something about the double bass and its influence in the symphony orchestra?

S.K.: The double bass is the one of the string family which is still most related to the old viols, which are the predecessors of the violins. This is evident in its shape, which is very often quite unlike the violins, insofar as it has no embellished edges and corners, a flat back, and is rather long in relation to its width. It is directly descended from the violone which was the double bass of the viol family. A double bass now can have either three, four or five strings, and only in very recent years has any system been adopted throughout the musical world of tuning the instrument. Even so, departures from the normal tuning systems are common. The double bass is usually tuned in fourths from the bottom string sounding E, the next string A, the next string

D and the next string G. On a five-stringed double bass they have an even lower string which is tuned to either B or C. Until steel strings were invented, the bass was noted for a particularly coarse sound.

A.S.: Solo repertoire is almost non-existent, isn't it?

S.K.: It consists of concertos written by bass players for themselves or their students; through the last 200 years odd pieces of music have been written for the double bass by good composers, obviously for some particular exponent of the instrument, but most of these players have proved untraceable. For instance, Dittersdorf wrote two concertos and Mozart wrote solos for the double bass—as I say, all for specific players.

A.S.: So you don't play the bass because of its rich solo repertoire; you play it for some other reason?

S.K.: I think that to play the bass for its solo repertoire is a complete waste of time. This is avoiding the idea of the bass entirely. The bass specifically is an orchestral instrument; solos can only be played for the amusement of the player.

A.S.: Is it particularly satisfying being at the bottom of the string chord in an orchestra? Is it possible to wield much influence from that position?

S.K.: Well, I've decided that, to be a bass player, you require a special sort of mentality, whereby you feel that what you are doing is of the utmost importance—and although it hasn't got the pleasures of the melodic lines of the violins, it still gives the player a great deal of pleasure, by contributing something which is so important to the harmonic structure.

A.S.: It is the biggest of all the instruments and quite heavy. Can girls play the bass?

S.K.: Oh, I have known several girls who play the double bass— two of them exceptionally fine players. It is not very heavy, it is only unwieldy to carry. The instrument actually weighs thirty to thirty-four pounds which isn't very heavy.

A.S.: How old would you have to be before you could even contemplate it?

S.K.: It is possible to start before twelve, but I was fifteen when I started to play.

A.S.: Can one start with a cello tuned as a bass, as a viola player sometimes starts on mistuned violins?

S.K.: Well, this is the rational beginning; I think the earlier one starts in music the better it is, because it is so easy to get past the drudgery when one is young.

A.S.: You mentioned that it is the last of the string family to have the viol form, but there are some basses, aren't there, that have the violin shape?

S.K.: Nearly violin shape. All basses have very sloping shoulders which are a characteristic of the viols.

A.S.: Your own instrument is violin-shaped.

S.K.: Well, it has the embellished corners of the violin, but on the other hand it has very sloping shoulders and a flat back.

A.S.: What is it? It looks a very beautiful one.

S.K.: It's a Magini: I am surprised you can see it under the dust!

A.S.: Is it worth a lot of money?

S.K.: Well, to me it's absolutely irreplaceable. I would imagine that its money value would be about £1,000.

A.S.: Could you offer any advice to someone who wanted to play the bass and would like to try it? Whom should they approach?

S.K.: The best person to approach is the nearest teacher of the cello. Most cellists feel that they have abilities on the bass—most of them have—and I am certain that the method used to teach the cello is by far the most effective way of learning the bass.

A.S.: What sort of a career is it in England, to be a bass player? Is the standard of playing very high?

S.K.: The highest standard of playing is in America and Czecho-slovakia, and of course the standard of tuition in those two countries is also exceptional. In England a different sort of standard is accepted, where experience and knowledge to a great extent outweigh specific virtuosity on the instrument.

A.S.: Are you interested in teaching?

S.K.: I like teaching. Not particularly the bass, but I am interested in teaching music generally.

A.S.: You never taught in one of the colleges of music?

S.K.: No. I disagree with the system of teaching which is accepted in these institutes. One is not prepared for a career as an outstanding musician. One is only taught to certain examination standards, which do nothing to assist the student. (You'll have to scrub all this lot out!) Surprisingly enough, quite a few remarkably good players do come out, but this in my opinion is always in spite of the system of tuition, rather than because of it. And one of the reasons for the tremendous shortage of good players in England is the system of tuition.

A.S.: Can you suggest any other approach?

S.K.: Yes, a very obvious one. Fifty years ago the standard of tuition in England was very high, and this was because conductors and various authorities used to import teachers from the Continent, and they brought with them their 'system'. Now we don't have so many foreign musicians in this country.

A.S.: If that is so, why do you think it is that London has so many orchestras—presumably of a good standard, because they are famous all over the world? How does that come about if the tuition is so lacking?

S.K.: In the first place, we have to analyse this. "London has so many orchestras presumably of a good standard." London has five orchestras, but the standard of at least three of them is very questionable. But whatever standard we have is attained by the fantastic enthusiasm of the people who are in the orchestras themselves; who work ridiculous hours and under ridiculous conditions, just because they like doing that, but the only instruments in which we have a particularly high standard are woodwind and certain of the brass instruments. We don't have a particularly high standard on any of the stringed instruments. What we have are sections which are enthusiastic, and therefore provide good results.

A.S.: Do you think the better standard of wind playing is in any way due to the military band and the brass band?

S.K.: Certainly not. The military bands and the brass bands are the establishments which have retarded the advancement of British wind playing, and the standard at this present stage is due solely to the virtuosity of one or two people of the previous generation who, by their own particular example, set a new standard in England.

A.S.: What sort of people are you thinking of?

S.K.: Archie Camden, Leon Goossens, Arthur Cleghorn, Reginald Kell and Jack Thurston. We had, I suppose, a couple of dozen outstanding woodwind players in the last generation, and they revolutionised playing in England.

A.S.: Will there always be a place for the Beethoven symphony orchestra as it exists today, if only to act as a sort of museum, performing eighteenth, nineteenth and twentieth century music?

S.K.: When one sees a statue by Michelangelo, or a painting by Rubens, or Van Dyck, one doesn't think one is looking at a museum piece; one knows one is looking at a masterpiece of human achievement. The symphonies of Beethoven, just as the music of Richard Strauss or Monteverdi, are equally masterpieces. A symphony orchestra doesn't evolve—the composers evolve. The orchestra is a vehicle for producing what the composer has achieved. The era of giganticism in the late nineteenth and early twentieth century is pretty well over, but still, when one performs some of the great works of Richard Strauss or Arnold Schoenberg, it is necessary to include such instruments as heckelphone, contra bass clarinet, octobasses and all these out-of-the-way instruments. It is still necessary to have them available. The orchestra for which Beethoven wrote will never become old-fashioned, any more than the hammer and chisel used by the great sculptors of the past will.

A.S.: As well as being principal bass, you are also Chairman of the Board of Directors: what does this involve? Is he a sort of figurehead?

'I enjoy the music, and the people I work with'.
Samuel Artis, violin with Ken Law, cello.

Some people have thought of past chairmen as 'Mr. L.S.O.'.

S.K.: As one thinks of Winston Churchill as Mr. Great Britain, or General de Gaulle as Mr. France, I suppose in any orchestra the boss tends to represent the "group"—as far as I am concerned, my job as Chairman of the Directors will be to try to influence the policy of the orchestra along the ways which I consider to be right for *music*. The end result of a symphony orchestra is the important thing. To improve fees, to improve standards, to improve concert halls is not the primary objective. If you have a good orchestra, you have a happy orchestra—you have a successful orchestra. If you give good concerts, you have happy and enthusiastic musicians, and I have very strong feelings about music, and if my ideals are wrong, it will be very quickly shown to me by the lack of support that I will have from my colleagues. I can only stand by what I think is right; if people agree with me I will be very happy.

A.S.: Can you think of any innovations that we ought to introduce?

S.K.: I think the most important thing is the encouragement of children's interest in music. Children are subject to a barrage of influences through the radio or television, and the ideals that the average child forms are a result of this propaganda—this brainwashing. The symphony orchestra, because it isn't a business venture, will of course be very lacking in self-advertisement on television and, as long as we don't get this propaganda on our behalf, we will be treated as something for other people to listen to, or as a sort of snob entertainment. In fact, music played by a symphony orchestra is just as thrilling as anything that the Beatles or any pop group has performed, and certainly of a much higher standard. What we have to do is find a way of presenting ourselves truthfully to young people, and this can only be done by television. At present television is the key to wider and new audiences, because it is the modern mass communication medium. You can't go a day without hearing the latest "Top of the Pops" ten or twelve times, no matter when you switch the machine on. If Beethoven's Ninth Symphony were pushed in a particular manner —and I'm not joking now—it would be just as popular.

A.S.: What can we do about it? How can the L.S.O. get this constant exposure to a new public?

S.K.: I can only say that the exposure has to be done through television. The way of doing it is something that experts in television will have to devise.

A.S.: What is the special quality that separates the L.S.O.?

S.K.: Fundamentally the special quality is that the standards of

'Generally, I think I have an ideal life.' ▶
Stuart Knussen, bass.

performance are the highest, and we have more people in the L.S.O. who want to give a high standard of performance than in any of the other London orchestras.

A.S.: Has that just come about by chance?

S.K.: I think it came about basically through the ideas of two men —John Cruft of the Arts Council and Harry Dugarde who was Chairman of the Board of Directors of the L.S.O. about twelve years ago. They were forced to face up to a situation where they needed to get new players in, and so, instead of picking up a series of established big musical names, they went around and searched for young men of talent with a result that the L.S.O. had a greater proportion of youthful talent than any of the other London orchestras.

A.S.: When players like Roger Lord, Gervase de Peyer and Barry Tuckwell joined the L.S.O.?

S.K.: Yes. Roger Lord was in the orchestra quite a bit before then, but, as you say, the people who originally came in, Roger Lord, Gervase de Peyer, Barry Tuckwell, Hugh McGuire—and it went on from there, and each year we still reap the benefit of the original attempt of these two people. Even this year we have got at least two great virtuosos into our orchestra, one a tuba player and one a cellist.

A.S.: And both quite young.

S.K.: Both of them very young. And again, the presence of these two young men will renew enthusiasm amongst the people already in the orchestra, and promote more interest in young players to come to our orchestra.

A.S.: What is the most enjoyable thing about being a member, principal bass, and Chairman of the Board of Directors of the L.S.O.?

S.K.: This is very easy. The most enjoyable thing about it all is that I am in the midst of a marvellous orchestra who are playing marvellous music most of the time. Some of the time I get a little bit disgruntled, if I don't like the music or something, but generally I think that I have an ideal life, because I'm doing something that I do very well, and something that I enjoy doing particularly well in all the circumstances.

If I was to be remembered, I would like to be remembered as a second Berlioz, but unfortunately I am not, so I know very well that I will not be remembered at all.

PART THREE

Woodwind

PETER LLOYD

Principal Flute

A.S.: How is it possible, Peter, to have two first flutes in a symphony orchestra? William Bennett and yourself.

P.L.: We are both on call whenever there are four flutes needed for a show—for the larger stuff, Mahler, Daphnis, any of the big things where there are four. We normally interchange; Wibb will play first for one session, and the next time I will. It is a very nice easy amicable arrangement and, provided that we don't both suddenly discover ourselves with concertos on the same day, the L.S.O. is perfectly happy. On those occasions we have to go to the personnel committee and beg them on our bended knees to release us both. It doesn't happen very often.

A.S.: You both put the L.S.O. work first?

P.L.: Well, of course. This is our main job; we both identify with the L.S.O. The work we do outside, we like to think, brings a certain amount of respect and maybe honour to the orchestra; it is not just a question of personal ambition.

A.S.: Are you pleased that you chose to play the flute?

P.L.: I was persuaded to play the flute when I first went to public school. My parents used to follow concerts, but apart from that there were no actual players in the family; they just thought it was a good idea for all of us three sons to take up some form of art at school. It was suggested that, as I was an asthmatic, maybe I should play a wind instrument. I chose the flute.

A.S.: Did playing the flute help your asthma?

P.L.: I have no idea at all; they say that if you have asthma as a child you generally grow out of it. I still find that if I have a tough concert ahead, with a lot of nervous playing, with things that I feel are on the edge or not a hundred per cent right or a hundred per cent perfect, this can bring it on. Needless to say, I have to take precautions —a nice little asthma spray!

A.S.: Since the days of Bach, has the mechanical design of the flute altered at all?

P.L.: Very much so; the great giant was Quantz who produced a large treatise on the flute in the eighteenth century. He also wrote some 300 flute concertos and a vast quantity of chamber music. His treatise is marvellous, and now there are several groups in Europe doing the baroque music of Quantz, Bach and all the rest on original instruments.

As far as the instrument is concerned, the biggest improvement came in the 1840s when Theobald Boehm started experimenting; he built a system of keys for the flute and completely revolutionised the whole thing—Quantz's flute had no keys, or, rather, just one on the bottom note and that was the lot. Boehm's system, perfected a bit later, is the one we now use.

A.S.: The great thing about our life in the L.S.O. is that it is terribly busy—do you have time for any hobbies?

P.L.: A certain amount. The trouble with hobbies is that they do take time. I like to play squash a certain amount to keep myself fit, but this is unfortunately not always possible. I find that to take up a sport like that one has got to be fit in the first place, otherwise you go tearing round the court and you would be on your back in no time.

A.S.: How many children have you got?

P.L.: Two children; two boys.

A.S.: Are they musical?

P.L.: The older one has started learning the piano; he is eight. He has been doing piano for six months and seems to be very quick. He has an excellent ear, and so I have fears that he might become interested in it, but I hope not professionally.

A.S.: Would you not encourage him to be a professional musician?

P.L.: I would never discourage them, from whatever they want to do.

A.S.: On balance do you think this is a good profession to be in?

P.L.: It is a very good young man's profession. When you are a young man, you think you have prospects if you are a good player; you get a chance, and you get into one of these big orchestras. It might take you a little while to get there. Fine! You get there, maybe in your thirties, but then you must realise that if you are an active orchestral musician, your earning powers and your capacity for keeping a good standard decline once you reach your fifties—particularly as a wind player. I know there are exceptions who manage to stick on until their eighties, but really I think for most of us we cannot expect to be good top class principals once we are just beyond fifty.

A.S.: And what will you do when you are beyond fifty?

P.L.: I hope to have the sense to drop to a second position, and that by that time I will have gone on improving my prospects of teaching. There should be good professionals in this country who are interested in teaching in the colleges, because after all it is only those people who know exactly what problems can be encountered in the profession.

A.S.: You find time to do some teaching now, don't you?

P.L.: I do six or seven hours a week at the Guildhall School of Music; Geoffrey Gilbert helped me there very much when I first came down here. I used to teach in Manchester with him, and when he came down here he helped me get a similar job at the Guildhall. I enjoy this very much. It takes up a lot of time; it is very difficult; it's hard work and sometimes one really wonders how one is going to get through the day when you make a flip of the diary and see another nine hours with the L.S.O. the next day, but somehow one does, and it's great fun.

A.S.: You said it is a young man's profession, and we sort of emphasise the youthfulness of the L.S.O. Do you think we overdo this a bit?

P.L.: Not the way that we work in London. I don't think that it would be possible for an older orchestra—say an orchestra with an average age in the late forties—to do the work that we do. There has got to be some reconstruction in the future of the way of employment of British orchestras, because we do have to work so hard to make the necessary living. If you take the case of the Berlin, or the big American orchestras, they work very very much less hours a week than we do; they get all their necessary pensions and holidays and all the rest, and they get a certain feeling of security. Here in London we don't get the feeling of security unless we are working jolly hard while we can.

A.S.: What about the other old chestnut about women in the orchestra? I know you have played in the Northern Orchestra, the Hallé and the Scottish National. They all have women and we know we are the last orchestra in England not to have women. Any comment?

P.L.: Yes. I think that I would rather the L.S.O. remained as it is. It is a more professional outfit as it is. Women can be a distraction. . . .

F

ROGER LORD

Principal Oboe

A.S.: As the leader of the woodwind section, you must have special problems, keeping things under control?

R.L.: At a rehearsal of the Fantastic Symphony some years ago we came to the woodwind chord marked poco forte at the start of the last movement and I played pretty well out, that is a little less than forte. I noticed that Mr. Gervase de Peyer was playing only a little more than piano, and so I turned round and volunteered the opinion that poco forte should be played louder than mezzo forte. Gervase disagreed, and I was surprised when he wouldn't give way one bit. If my memory doesn't play me false, we did not ask for a casting vote from the conductor, and no doubt in the performance in the evening we came to a truly British compromise.

This is always a tricky question, whether to ask the conductor or not. There's always the chance that he will not be on your side, or that he will want to be so diplomatic that he will try to prove you both right, and you find yourselves back where you started.

I held to my views about poco forte until wonderful fresh light was cast on the subject when we came to the Slow Movement of Brahms' Fourth Symphony, one day, when Pierre Monteux was conducting. If you remember, cellos and violas are marked pf. With winning charm and a mischievous smile, and thoroughly delighted with himself, Monteux said to the cellos—who have the tune: 'Poco FORTE!' and then, turning to the violas: 'POCO forte'. How right he was, and it is remarkable how many things in music depend on this sort of interpretation.

That is one reason why it is no good allowing one's views to become too fixed, particularly in an orchestra like the L.S.O., where we play under many different conductors. We have the opportunity to learn a great deal about interpretation and, as a result, to sift out what we each consider the most desirable way of playing something. The conductor has to weld all our ideas into one by convincing us that he knows best. We have to keep a fairly open mind about things and, if we do our job properly, we will sound convincing even if we find ourselves playing in a manner quite different from our individual ideal. Afterwards we have the opportunity to revise our ideas, depending on the success or otherwise of the interpretation. There is no one way, which is why music is so fascinating in performance.

A.S.: That deals with dynamics; what about the thorny question of intonation?

R.L.: What one must bear in mind is that when playing chords in the woodwind, one is trying to blend notes of several *different* colours, which is quite a lot more difficult than blending notes of the same colour, as in purely string chords or brass chords. Not only this, there is also the matter of the imperfections inherent in certain instruments, particularly in—dare I say it?—the clarinet, where bringing one register of the instrument up to pitch will throw out another register, so that the only answer is a compromise, which has to be compensated for by the player, either by 'fingering' or the lip.

Playing in certain keys is more difficult than others as far as intonation is concerned. For some reason or other the flat keys are easier than the sharp ones. E major is a devil—witness the opening chords of Midsummer Night's Dream Overture, or Scheherazade, which can make a disastrous start to a concert if one player alone is a little bit nervous or unsure of himself.

It is not just a question of pitch. A chord can sound very wrong just because it is ill-balanced. Beethoven presents his own problems because of his habit of doubling up thirds and fifths through the octaves, thereby giving his own particular sonority, but inviting various degrees of sourness. And of course when you are sitting *in* the woodwind section, it is more difficult to hear what is wrong than when listening from outside the group. That is why it is sometimes annoying when a conductor says: 'It's flat, or sharp, or something!'—even if he rightly considers that it is the players' job to put things right.

Van Beinum was a fine orchestral trainer and he never hesitated—when there was time—to 'build up' a woodwind chord from the bottom, starting with the second bassoon and on through the clarinets, oboes and flutes, adding fifths and octaves and lastly thirds, until the sound was perfect. He always made sure, though, that the fundamental itself was *down* to pitch, because a sharp fundamental makes everything else sound sour.

Sharpness always sounds better than flatness, which is why players like to be on the bright side. Oh, the joys of having tuning-pegs like the strings, and being able to slide the fingers just a little further up the fingerboard to score yet another little bit of one-upmanship! But how silly it sounds when the open strings have to be played, as happens now and again. Still, you can always make a big show of tuning down, and then tune up again when the hoo-ha has died down.

The other day when we played the pianoforte version of the

Beethoven Violin Concerto, I was wondering why I was reminded of the Emperor Concerto so much, apart from the obvious similarities in passage-work and so on. Then I realised what it was. At the end of the orchestral tuttis, the piano solo would come in just a little bit flat. Now no violin soloist would ever do that, but the poor pianist can't do anything about it.

One of my oboe player friends was once given a bottle of Scotch by Isaac Stern in return for giving a sharp A before the concerto. So far I haven't been that lucky!

A.S.: What about the actual quality of woodwind tone? A wide range of tonal colours is possible on all woodwind instruments, isn't it?

R.L.: A player should be able to produce what I call a positive sound and a negative sound, and various degrees in between. This is only partly to do with loudness and softness, and by negative I do not mean a dead sound. The positive sound is used for solos or rather when you have the lead, and you 'negate' the sound—by reducing its brightness and penetrating qualities—when you are accompanying or getting out of the way of another player whose part is more important than yours. And if you don't do this you are not doing your job properly!

This 'producing the right sort of sound' helps with the balancing of chords, but sometimes a player is having to produce a note, perhaps at the bottom of the oboe register or at the top of the clarinet, where the amount of control is limited and he is unable to play as pianissimo as his more fortunate colleagues who are playing in easier registers. The players must then produce a little more sound all round in order to help the unfortunate one from sticking out like the proverbial sore thumb. Sometimes in Mozart works, when the wind-band consists of oboes and horns only, the horn parts can be quite high. The oboe players can not only make life miserable for the horns but ruin the effect if they don't give solid support—albeit with a dolce sound—in the oboe/horn chords, and produce a balanced effect.

A.S.: And of course the woodwind choir must be together, both with themselves and with the rest of the orchestra?

R.L.: You look at the conductor. His beat comes down. When do you come in? At the bottom of the beat. What if there is some doubt about where the bottom of the beat is? You come in at the moment when, if you wait any longer, it will be too late. (This is not as silly as it sounds: whether you think you are using extra-sensory perception or just being aware of the players around you, such a moment does exist.) In other words it will be too late in relation to the music and to

◄ *'A bottle of Scotch for giving a sharp A.'*
Roger Lord, oboe.

the other instruments that are coming in with you. If a string player has one pizzicato plink to make at the same time as the whole brass choir comes in with a Wagnerian-type chord, he's going to find himself playing a solo if he doesn't restrain his ardour, even if the Maestro has not only reached the bottom of the beat but is beginning to look panic-stricken into the bargain. Being aware of what is going on apart from your own part is very important most of the time.

I say most of the time because sometimes when we are making stereo records or working in the T.V. studios with the orchestra widely spread out, almost in separate little camps, it is of vital importance to play by eye alone and not by ear, otherwise aural time-lag causes trouble. On such occasions it is almost better if we are unaware of what else is going on!

On the other hand, when two solo instruments are playing the same line, the conductor's beat, however clear, may not be sufficient to keep them absolutely together, and the rule then is for the player who can most easily hear his colleague to 'play the reflection in the mirror'.

The other day a conductor observed that one only heard what went on in front of one, and no-one took him up on it. I think that was because he said it with great charm—you can get away with a great deal by this means, and what a good thing it is. I would point out that if I have a tune to play in unison with the first trumpet, I know I have to 'ghost' him, because he cannot hear me at all when he is playing, whereas I can hear him, although—and partly because—he is seated behind me. Similarly in Debussy's Fêtes I have to rely on the principal viola doing his best to hang on to me when we play together, because I cannot hear him, and I am lucky if I can see his bow on account of the number of giants we have in the L.S.O. viola section!

Woodwinds—Roger Lord and Harry Lythell, oboes

GERVASE DE PEYER
Principal Clarinet

A.S.: You have been principal clarinet of the London Symphony Orchestra for years and years now, as long as I can remember. In fact, Gervase, you were one of the new principals when the Sinfonia of London broke away from the old London Symphony weren't you?

G. de P.: Yes, I was. The crisis arose I think over the clarinet player; clarinet players seem to get into this sort of trouble. A lot of the old guard of the L.S.O. offered their resignations in support of the previous principal clarinet and, rather to everybody's astonishment and theirs, their resignations were accepted and their places were gradually filled by young musicians, of which I suppose I could name myself the first.

A.S.: Were you playing second clarinet or something?

G. de P.: No, no. I was playing in other orchestras in London and doing free-lance work and so on.

A.S.: And really the quality that the L.S.O. is now known for stems from that time?

G. de P.: It was some time before the orchestra actually pulled up, before its standards really improved and before it was recognised that they had—you know, the one always follows the other rather at a distance. The orchestra got better and it also coincided, up to a point, with Ernest Fleischman's approach to management at that time; he came in as the new General Secretary, and he did a great deal to put forward the image which the orchestra still has, of being a very keen, young, dynamic organisation; quite a different thing from what it had been before.

A.S.: So you have seen the L.S.O. from the inside over a number of years; how do you like the way things have gone recently?

G. de P.: I think the playing standards have gone steadily upwards, and I think that it's just as well that they have, because undoubtedly five years ago the orchestra was probably then one of the best orchestras in London. Perhaps there is one other which one could mention as well, but recently—particularly recently, I think—the other orchestras

(Overleaf): 'It is a very good young man's profession.'
Peter Lloyd, flute.

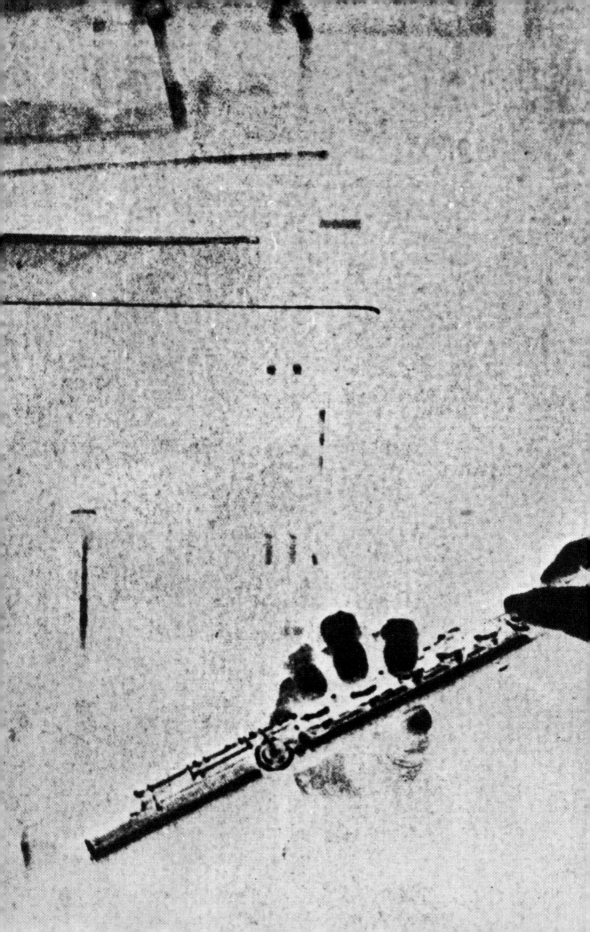

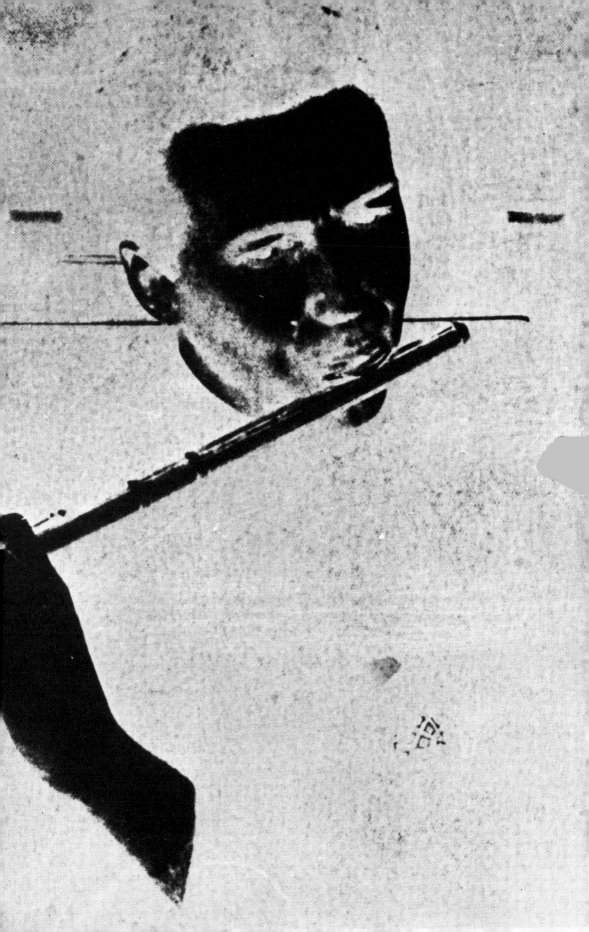

have come up, so it's just as well that the London Symphony has too! Otherwise talk might have been going around that the orchestra was slipping and that the others were coming to take the crown of the virtuoso orchestra of London. That sort of thing can happen very easily, but I think that the L.S.O. can still hold its head up quite proudly and fear nobody.

A.S.: How old were you when you first met the clarinet?

G. de P.: I was about twelve; you know, like many others, I took it up in order to play it while I was at school.

A.S.: You have waged a sort of crusade for the solo clarinet repertoire, haven't you?

G. de P.: Well, yes. It's very difficult for wind players to establish themselves as soloists in the same way that string players and pianists can. It's partly because of repertoire, although that angle isn't so important; the repertoire isn't rich enough perhaps in great concertos to make it possible to go around just playing those as a soloist, like certain pianists and violinists can do. On the other hand, I've always maintained, and still do, that a lot of the concertos that there *are* are much better than people think; my experience has been that when I'm allowed to play anything, like Weber for instance, instead of the usual Mozart, they've often gone down better than the Mozart. I mustn't say that they are better pieces, but they have a more dynamic appeal to an audience.

A.S.: You've played an enormous number of concertos with the L.S.O., haven't you, over the years?

G. de P.: I have played a lot of concertos round the world, but I would hesitate to suggest that I had been asked to do this in preference to a popular piano soloist or to a popular violinist. I think that sometimes it's convenient to have somebody who is going to be on the tour anyway playing a concerto. But if it's been a question of getting a big draw to sell out a big hall or something—well, a violinist or a pianist usually can do it better than me, can't he?

A.S.: You started the clarinet when you were twelve; is that about the right age to begin do you think?

G. de P.: Oh no, I don't think so, I mean you can start it earlier than that, possibly start it later. You know, a real youngster can start on some of the mini clarinets, in E Flat or B or something like that; one or two youngsters that I know have done just that and I think it's probably as much of a help as it is to take up anything when one's very young—like ballet-dancing or playing the piano. If you start it very young, and you get some decent teaching, I think it does help; I think that twelve is reasonable enough. But I didn't really concentrate on the clarinet for many years—not until I'd finished thinking I might be a pianist.

A.S.: The initial stages of a clarinet are encouraging, aren't they? You can make a nice sound quite quickly?

G. de P.: You can make a sound quite quickly—I don't think you can necessarily make a nice sound!

A.S.: There is one big advantage to a young person playing a clarinet—when he has reached a certain standard he has the opportunity to play chamber music and orchestral music which he wouldn't have with a piano.

G. de P.: That's why I took it up, in fact; I was asked to take up an instrument and I took up the clarinet because I thought the repertoire was the best. I think I'd heard the Clarinet Quintet of Brahms or Mozart and liked it and that decided me.

A.S.: How much does a clarinet cost?

G. de P.: They vary from £20 to £130 or even more if you are going to buy one of the foreign ones with tax. But the best one made in this country is between £120 and £130.

A.S.: What do you play on at the moment?

G. de P.: I play on the last kind; it's a Boosey and Hawkes 1010 clarinet which actually is fairly new—it's only two years old. A lot of American players are expressing interest now in English clarinets and the English way of playing—and the instrument is partly responsible for this. It's more mellifluous, more subtle, I think. In France and America clarinet playing particularly tends to be rather stiff and the thought of actually floating a sound is something which they don't seem to be able to do. They either cut with it, or hammer with it, or something of the sort. But actually floating it so that the sound has got subtlety and the sort of suppleness of the human voice seems not to have occured to them. You should be able to do that on a clarinet. I can never think of woodwind playing at all without relating it to singing, to the human voice.

A.S.: Do you see the principal clarinet in the orchestra and in the woodwind section as in any special role? Are there any special difficulties or pitfalls?

G. de. P.: Yes: I think that it does on the whole rest with one or two artists to set a standard which other people can try to live up to or try to emulate. In any orchestra these things are catching up to a point. Everybody pretends that everybody else is just doing a routine job and you can do something very beautifully and nobody says anything; equally one hopes that you can do something extremely badly and no-one will say anything either! This is a sort of tactful professionalism at work.

A.S.: Do you find it discouraging when you feel you've played something beautifully and people don't say anything because there is this sort of professional taboo? Does that upset you?

G. de P.: No, I don't mind them not saying at all, but it would hurt me if I thought they hadn't noticed, and I very often think they haven't. I mean, not particularly when I've played something I was rather proud of, but when somebody else has as well. You know, I do think that it's easy for players in an orchestra to develop cloth ears—things just get soaked up and don't impinge, don't make any impression. Because all the players in an orchestra are listening to so many notes and so much music all the time, it's impossible to actually concentrate enough very often to be able to judge whether something was absolutely first class or whether it was just all right.

A.S.: The clarinet is very much a solo instrument in classical, romantic and certainly modern music, so you are always sticking your neck out, so to speak. Do you ever regret that you are playing such an instrument and that you are not one of a team of twelve or fifteen, sixteen?

G. de P.: Well now, the sort of team you are talking of in fact means being a string player, doesn't it? And I don't think I would like that at all!

A.S.: Why not?

G. de P.: Because I'm not that sort of person. You know, I don't like to play something, for instance, and not be able to hear quite accurately what I am playing. That's just the first thing. And the other thing is that I do tend on the whole to think that my way of doing something is right and if somebody sitting next to me is doing the same piece that I'm doing and doing it differently, I'm sure it would irritate me to death.

A.S.: What is your favourite repertoire to play in the symphony orchestra? Are there certain concerts you really look forward to?

G. de P.: No. I don't look forward like that to a particular repertoire because for me it's not simply a question of a certain piece being a favourite; it's also a question, in a concert, of that certain piece being performed in a way which really is going to give me pleasure. I can get enormous pleasure out of taking part in Mozart or Beethoven or Haydn symphonies for instance if, and this happens very rarely for me, I feel that they are really being performed extremely well. If it's not, I wish I was conducting it myself and that I wasn't there playing at all.

A.S.: You must look forward with longing to the Slow Movement of, say, the Rachmaninov Second Symphony, the clarinet tune in that.

G. de P.: Yes—if one has got a really lovely melody or a lovely tune, it is nice to play it. There is a marvellous clarinet solo in The Trojans which is the most wonderful thing. Unfortunately I've only ever had to play it once, because I've been away, not available most of the times when the orchestra's played it. But when I did play it, I think it was at the Albert Hall Promenade or something, I enjoyed it thoroughly. And there are things like that which are marvellous to play.

A.S.: Are there any things that worry you in the repertoire?

G. de P.: Oh yes, everything: I mean everything can be worrying. It's very much a question of how one is on that particular day; whether one's got a reed, or whether one's fit, or something like that.

A.S.: Where do you get your reeds from?

G. de P.: I get mine from France, same as most people here, Vandoren reeds.

A.S.: Do you finish them yourself?

G. de P.: Oh, I fiddle about with them myself, yes. A lot. And I've got a sort of machine at home which helps me, and I use endless grades of abrasive papers and knives and whatnots, you know.

A.S.: What about plastic ones? Do you use those?

G. de P.: I have done. I remember a lamentable occasion when I tried using a glass fibre one at a concert in the Albert Hall.

A.S.: What happened?

G. de P.: Well, it wasn't until the actual concert that I realised that I wasn't going to be able to get through because it was such hard work to actually play it. I put it on in the band room. Things are very misleading there and so I had to sort of hastily take it off in mid-performance of one of the most notorious of Beethoven's symphonies—the Eighth which has got a difficult thing to play in the trio.

A.S.: It's got a High F.

G. de P.: That's right; I had to put on my old wooden one, having played the First Movement of the symphony on a glass fibre one. And I found that the wooden one had dried out and become like they sometimes do when they dry out—they warp and get like corrugated iron, rather than a straight reed. Of course, you know, it didn't work at all well with, I thought, disastrous results. Dear old Sir Malcolm Sargent gave me a very sweet smile at the end of it, so perhaps it wasn't as bad as I'd thought.

A.S.: Actually, you have got a bit of a reputation as a conductor-baiter. Do conductors annoy you?

G. de P.: No. I mean actually I find myself rather in sympathy with conductors if two things about them are true: one is that they are genuinely trying to do a good job; and the other is that they are humble enough to realise when they are not. And the type of conductor who is either so blind or conceited that he can't see that he is making life more difficult for people in the orchestra by just not being clear or not being precise or whatever is very annoying to me. And also the kind of conductor who seems to be using the music or the players as a means to further his career without any genuine feel for the music. I'm quite prepared to put up with quite a bad conductor without saying anything if I feel the chap is really sincere, that really he has got his heart in the right place and he is prepared to be helped as well as to try and help.

But the ones who don't seem to want any help or be prepared to accept any—who, indeed, are incapable of believing that they could possibly benefit by any—really I find them very hard.

A.S.: And you express it sometimes . . . But you are joining their ranks now?

G. de P.: Yes, I am; because, you know, I've always felt that I had rather clearer ideas myself as to how I'd like the music to go. But actually in the performance of music I have felt over the years that I can get things out which do make some sort of an impact on the public. I mean, I've done it in chamber music a lot and then, when I started conducting, I had a few shocks in overcoming the initial difficulties of being at the giving end rather than the receiving end, in mastering the conductor/orchestra relationship. But I found that that quickly sorted itself out and, although I'm certainly far from being an experienced conductor, I do feel that, given a reasonably fair chance, I could do it as well, or perhaps a little bit better, than some.

RONALD MOORE

Clarinet

A.S.: Ronnie, what is your position with the L.S.O. in the clarinet section?

R.M.: I'm the second clarinet and also play the E flat when required.

A.S.: The E flat is the smaller one which has quite important and often exposed solos, isn't it?

R.M.: Yes, that's right. Sometimes it's called the clarinetto piccolo.

A.S.: How did you come to fall into this job? Were you ever an ordinary first clarinet? How does one gravitate to these more obscure regions of the orchestra?

R.M.: When I was invited to join the orchestra it was also put to me that I should buy myself an E flat clarinet and learn to play it as part of the job, which I undertook to do. But I think clarinettists in general feel themselves attracted towards other members of the clarinet family like the bass clarinet—sometimes they find they happen to be good on them—so they make a specialised job of it.

A.S.: It's rare to be able to play the E flat, the A and B flat—that's the usual pair of clarinets—and the bass clarinet equally well. Does that ever happen?

R.M.: Yes, it is rather rare, but I can think of one or two people who can do this. It's not very usual.

A.S.: In one concert you yourself might be called upon to play the A and B flat and possibly the small piccolo E flat clarinet as well.

R.M.: Yes. It does happen that I sometimes have to play all three. It isn't an ideal state of affairs because if you are going to produce absolutely your best on any one instrument you have certain problems because you have to adjust your embouchure, your mouth muscles, to a particular sized mouthpiece and you can't really dodge from one to the other and expect to produce top class results from all.

A.S.: That's true in the strings, too; violinists can't change to viola overnight.

R.M.: And we have the added hazard that, for ideal results, to play on more than one instrument we must have identical types of reed.

A.S.: The reed problem is the nightmare problem for all woodwind players, isn't it?

R.M.: Yes, I'm afraid it is. Although as a clarinettist I hear all my colleagues grumbling about the inferior quality of reeds I think that one's other colleagues on the double reed instruments such as the oboe and bassoon have an additional problem because they've got to find two bits of cane which function nicely together and we've only got to find one. Mind you we have mouthpieces to grumble about as well.

A.S.: Most of your work with the L.S.O. is as second clarinet. Are there any special problems associated with playing second?

R.M.: Yes, there certainly are. To be a good second clarinet, one has to be extremely flexible musically and one has to try and merge oneself with the personality of one's principal without becoming absolutely faceless oneself. It's not always easy.

A.S.: We have two principal clarinettists—Gervase and Roy Jowitt. Do you have to make special adjustments to each of their styles?

R.M.: Yes, I find I do. One of them might attack entries at a slightly different moment of time to the other.

A.S.: Surely the attack is indicated by the conductor's beat.

R.M.: In theory it is, but the conductor's beat is something that one always has to take with a pinch of salt and you weigh up for yourself whether you are going to take this conductor absolutely seriously as far as his indications are concerned. Some people like to give a very precise beat and you feel it's going to be helpful to follow him, but with others

—let's face it, you can't follow them usually. You have to arrive at some sort of a compromise.

A.S.: Does that sort of a compromise really work with a complex orchestra—not following a conductor's beat—doesn't it result in a shambles?

R.M.: No, funnily enough, not always. There are some conductors who appear to be able to give a very followable beat and yet the orchestra will sound a shambles.

A.S.: Who are they?

R.M.: I'm not going to mention any names, I'm afraid.

A.S.: Which conductors do you find have a very clear precise beat—which ones do you admire?

R.M.: So far as a clear and precise beat is concerned, coupled with what I think is a most advanced state of musicianship, then I think Rozhdestvensky is the man. I think it's quite remarkable the way he is able to identify himself exactly with what is going on in any piece of music. Sometimes one doesn't get that precision, but one does get the musicianship and you don't really always need such a precise beat.

A.S.: That pre-supposes a lot of experience on the part of the players.

R.M.: Oh, it does. There is no doubt that an orchestra that plays a long time with more or less the same personnel does acquire a remarkable ability to play most things together without much help.

A.S.: To what extent, then, does a conductor stamp a performance with his personality?

R.M.: The conductor is very important because, although we very often have our own good musical ideas, somebody has got to co-ordinate these ideas into a whole. After all, if an orchestra plays together and it plays in tune and it plays in good balance, this is half the battle. If the conductor can also add a sort of excitement to the performance, enthusiasm, which many of them can do—this is what distinguishes a good performance from a routine performance.

A.S.: As a part of that performance—playing a subordinate role—do you ever feel frustrated?

R.M.: Occasionally, but not very often. One inevitably has one's own private feelings about how something should be played. The day one doesn't have those feelings, perhaps, one ought to give up playing. I don't feel myself really dying to get hold of the first clarinet part, if that's what you mean.

A.S.: You don't think that the enormous amount of work that you do on committees and as a director of the orchestra is in any way a

'A sub-principal's life is probably much longer.'
Ronald Moore, clarinet. ▶

substitute for the extra amount of responsibility you might have were you a principal player?

R.M.: If I were a principal I would certainly not do any of the work I now do on committees. To keep up the sort of standard that is expected in this orchestra requires such attention to detail from a principal player that it would not be possible. A sub-principal's life is probably very much longer.

A.S.: How is it that you are able to cope with that nightmarish solo in Till Eulenspiegel with such monotonous perfection? Have you studied that particular piece?

R.M.: I have in fact turned it practically inside out, and myself as well; I always without exception feel extremely nervous about it whenever we play it. If I stopped caring about it, it would start going to pieces. I have to get worked up about it every time.

A.S.: As well as Gervase de Peyer and Roy Jowitt, sometimes you play with the other distinguished clarinet principals in London. Have you got a favourite?

R.M.: Um . . .! You flummox me now, because there are so many different styles of clarinet playing that one can appreciate them all— and some of them suit different styles of music better than others. When one is playing with a principal who has a solo, say, in front of him to which he is particularly suited, then it's marvellous. This applies to them all. They are all good at particular things and not so good at others. But the job of actually playing with them is more a question of absorbing their particular way of giving expressive nuance on the clarinet which varies from player to player. Although one can't do very much to alter one's own natural sound I tend to veer towards the sound of the person I am playing with as far as I can. If some of them produce a more brilliant sound than others, then I try to produce a more brilliant sound; if they produce a more smooth, darker sound, then I shall try and do the same. This is what a second clarinet should do.

A.S.: If you know you are to play with a given principal player, are you able to predict with any accuracy the sort of phrasing he will use because you know his playing from experience?

R.M.: Yes, I certainly can do this. This is part of the art, I suppose— being able to guess in advance what is going to happen. It's artistic instinct, I suppose, more than anything else.

ROGER BIRNSTINGL
Principal Bassoon

A.S.: Roger, your name is very unusual, where do you come from?

R.B.: Well, the family comes from, and they were born in, England. The name is Austrian, but my great-great-grandfather came from Arad, which is now in Romania. There were two brothers who left the country in 1848 during a cholera epidemic and, after a period in Australia, settled respectively in Paris and London, the one being a watch maker and the other, the London brother, a photographer—we have photographs of his shop in Bond Street and a lot of photographs taken by him which are really incredibly good.

A.S.: How old were you when you started the bassoon?

R.B.: I was about fourteen.

A.S.: That is quite late really to start, isn't it?

R.B.: I had worked very hard at the piano, you see. I had all sorts of romantic ideas about being a pianist and I used to get all gooey about films like *The Seventh Veil*; James Mason saying: 'Well, if you won't play for me, you won't play for anyone'—Bang!

A.S.: Do you still play the piano?

R.B.: When I can find time.

A.S.: Have you had many regrets over deciding to be a bassoonist?

R.B.: No, I have never had any regrets at all about it. I was very lucky because almost before I had even finished three years at college, I was playing in the Philharmonia—well now the Philharmonia in those day swas undoubtedly the finest orchestra in London, and I joined just at the time they were going to America. This was, I think, the second British orchestra to go to America since the war; Karajan was conducting and every musician in London wanted to go on that tour. The result was that the orchestra had a string section that was unique; everyone was either a string quartet leader or chamber music player of a calibre which you don't normally see altogether in one orchestra. And they really played for Karajan. Of course, I was very impressionable at that time, so it all seemed to me that that was something which we were never going to hear again; I hope I was wrong. But certainly at that time it seemed to me to be an absolutely wonderful life!

A.S.: Of course, one's standards do change as one gets older.

R.B.: Well I think so, because for one thing you hear things for the first time when you are young and everything seems to be so exciting. Later you hear more behind the music, but the actual spontaneity of your musical appreciation is slightly less acute and this is very sad.

A.S.: Since those days other orchestras have been to America. Actually in 1912 the L.S.O. was the first orchestra that ever went to America and since then we have been back almost once a year. Do you find these visits interesting and exciting?

R.B.: I have always enjoyed touring and when I had the chance, that is to say, when I was free-lancing and wasn't attached to an orchestra, I used to manage about four or five different tours in a year. There was one year when I went to Russia, America, Japan, Sicily and Italy, all in one year, and that was a very normal thing. I can never do too much sight-seeing, and I was always in the fortunate position of not having a family or anything to worry about . . . it didn't really make any difference to me whether I was in London or somewhere else, I just made the best of it.

A.S.: What about now, do you still like it?

R.B.: Oh yes, I still love touring. I wouldn't want to tour all the time, by any means, but I certainly enjoy going anywhere in the world. There are always interesting things to see.

A.S.: You are a home-lover as well. You have obviously taken a lot of interest in this magnificent flat of yours, so you must like the idea of being at home?

R.B.: I like to have my roots somewhere, it is true, but I would hate to spend the whole time just beautifying a little nest somewhere in London, though I wouldn't contemplate living in England as a musician in any other city than London. Everything goes on in London, like the theatre and opera, which I go to as much as I am able to; there just isn't anything outside London—it is a tragedy, really, but that is how it is. And I like London itself and I like the sort of cosmopolitan life. I am interested in art and pictures; I love to go to galleries and look at pictures—not that I am particularly knowledgeable.

A.S.: Boulez said yesterday that unless something is done to freshen up concert programmes symphony concerts will die. Can you think what he meant by that?

R.B.: But I think any form of art will become moribund if it's not always progressing, and if concerts just settle down into the old

Roger Birnstingl, bassoon. ▶

scheme of Sunday Albert Hall concerts, God help us all. Not that these concerts are poor music, but I think you have got to introduce new works all the time and try to decide which works really do want to be pushed before the public. There is no doubt about it—this is everybody's experience—hearing a work for the first time, you don't get a lot out of it. You just say: 'Little bits of that I quite liked, but I'm not really sure. I'd like to hear it again.' Well, for God's sake let's give them the chance to hear it again. And I think that it's the job of a promoter to tell whether a composer is writing music which is of any importance and, if it is, then it should be presented before the public as much as possible. But naturally this has got to be balanced against the box office; you have somehow got to slot it in in such a way that the concert-goer does hear it—without really noticing it. He buys his ticket even though he doesn't realise he's going to hear something rather difficult.

A.S.: Some people are put off going to concerts because they are a bit stuffy. Do we have to wear a white tie and tails? Does that matter?

R.B.: Well I think it does matter a bit. I go for instance to the opera at Covent Garden. To me it's quite an occasion. I mean, here is Covent Garden, which is a beautiful opera house from the inside and there is all this gold leaf around, lots of bright lights and lovely tabs, the curtains there, and it's all a little bit of a thrill and an anticipation. And there is the orchestra warming up. Well, I think that the least that the public can do, as a sort of gesture to the occasion, is to put on a decent suit or wear a nice dress or something. And these people who insist on going to Covent Garden dressed in old jeans and a filthy sweater—I would throw them out or put them well out of the way up in the gallery slips or something. I'm not suggesting that they shouldn't go because they haven't got decent clothes, but I think anyone who can should dress for the occasion. Well now, in the concert hall I think people should dress properly as well. I don't like seeing people turning up in rags and as far as the orchestra is concerned, I think it would be terrible if we all started turning up in polo-neck sweaters. However, I do think that there is certain music where one could possibly relax the ruling about wearing evening dress—if you are doing a concert such as I did this summer in Edinburgh— Le Renard by Stravinsky. We wore polo-neck sweaters for that and I think this was right; this somehow went with the music. But if you are going to play a classical programme, I think one should dress for it suitably.

A.S.: Can we come to the bassoon, your instrument in the symphony orchestra. I suppose the bassoon is the anchor man for the woodwind quartet, isn't he?—the bass part most of the time. Does this involve any special problems or responsibilities? For instance, intonation: does that come from the bassoon?

R.B.: Yes, very much. The second bassoon player is certainly of the utmost importance because the whole choir of the woodwind instruments is built up on this lowest instrument. He is usually for all intents and purposes at the bottom of all the chording. And if that isn't in tune, nothing is going to be in tune, so he is a very important member of the section.

But the first bassoon is in a different position because he is either helping out the second bassoon and forming the bass of this choir, or else he is definitely in the tenor position, and as such can be very much a soloist.

A.S.: Surely it's a bit frustrating playing expressive solos on the bassoon? Does it have a limited range of colours?

R.B.: No, it doesn't really; it has a very wide range—almost the greatest range of any wind instrument apart from the clarinet.

A.S.: You mean of pitch?

R.B.: Well, from the bottom to the top, it's $3\frac{1}{2}$ octaves and over, it has very different qualities of tone colour. And I think that the sort of effect that it can get in, for instance the beginning of the Rite of Spring, is something which could not be done by any other instrument. This eerie feeling of early morning, the sun just rising over the rite which is going to take place.

A.S.: What other composers write well for the bassoon?

R.B.: Mozart writes consistently, fabulously for the bassoon, I think.

A.S.: And after that?

R.B.: Well after that you could mention a lot of people, but someone who perhaps wouldn't spring to mind with everybody is Verdi. I think Verdi writes superbly for the bassoon. For a lot of the time he is just doing tonic-dominant stuff, just as a good many of the poor bass instruments are in Verdi operas, but suddenly he will do something absolutely magnificent and you feel the bassoon is exactly right for this. The Verdi Requiem has a huge obbligato for the bassoon which I think is one of the most satisfying things you can play as a bassoon player.

A.S.: When was the bassoon first written for in an orchestra?

R.B.: I'm not absolutely certain about that one, because composers used to write just a continuo bass line, and it was very much left to the discretion of the players how they filled in that continuo. It would have been for a harpsichord; for a violone, which is a sort of double bass; and probably for a bassoon if there happened to be a player around. I'm now talking of about the time of early baroque music. Bach has written for it specifically; there is a solo part in the First Brandenberg Concerto in one of the trios and he has specified that it should be played on the bassoon and nothing else.

A.S.: What did it evolve from?

R.N.: It is a member of the oboe family and thus you can really say

—in rehearsal, full orchestra.

that it has much the same antecedence as the oboe—it came from the shawm family, which is still extant today in Barcelona; the main characteristic of this family is that it is played with a double reed made from bamboo. This of course is the bane of every reed-player's life, because however many times you run round Hampstead Heath or however many times you have played squash, however much practice you have done and although you have got all your fingers really moving, it's absolutely useless if you haven't got a reed that's going to give the goods. For some reason it hasn't been possible to find a man-made substitute for this cane. They have in fact tried, but the point is they aren't prepared to do sufficient research into it to find a substance, some sort of nylon or something, which will do it as well as a natural fibre.

A.S.: Why is it such a personal thing—why is it that a good reed for one person wouldn't do for another?

R.B.: Yes, this is absolutely true. I think it is as personal as the sound you make on an instrument, and a superlative player can pick up a £5-clarinet and make it sound like their own £150-instrument.

A.S.: What is it that wind players are doing in rehearsals when they are not playing—sitting there with knives and little boxes and things?

R.B.: Scraping reeds; they have either bought or made a reed and they have brought it up to a certain sort of finish, which is, however, very far from what is actually needed to do a concert. If you are at home in your sitting room and you play an instrument, you are playing presumably in a rather small room and the sort of sound you get in that confined space doesn't really show you at all what it's going to sound like in a concert hall. In fact, by experience you get to know to some extent what is needed at home, but you usually find when you come to play in a big concert hall that the sound is not at all what you thought it was. So the only solution is to do your final touch up on the reed in situ—where you are going to actually do the concert. One of the most satisfying halls in London to play in so far as I am concerned is the Wigmore Hall. You can put any reed on your instrument in the Wigmore Hall and it sounds good because this is a wonderful hall—it has a natural resonance. It just doesn't matter what you do, it always sounds good there. While the Festival Hall is an absolute misery because if you have a poor reed, my God, you can hear it.

A.S.: Is there a shortage of bassoons? Are they readily available? How much do they cost?

R.B.: Um . . . The reason I am hesitating in answering that question is because there is really not a lot of difficulty in getting bassoons but it is precisely the cost which is the trouble. You have to pay between £130 and £150 to get a passable instrument even for a student.

A.S.: It's better if it's new is it?

Peter Francis, contra bassoon.

R.B.: No, not at all. I think it really isn't relevant how old an instrument is, it's just the condition it's in.

A.S.: Does it improve with age?

R.B.: No. I think a very new instrument is liable to change a bit because if the wood is fairly new it settles down over a few years and it can change; in a way I would advise people to buy an instrument which is several years old—say five years old, because if it's good when it's five years old, the chances are that it will stay in that state.

A.S.: What is the wood?

R.B.: Well, on most bassoons it is maple which is a very light coloured wood—not at all the colour that you think, looking at a bassoon; you think it's quite a dark wood, but that's only the varnishing. To see the colour of the wood you have to look inside the bore and it's very light, colour and weight-wise. And that's why it's used.

A.S.: Do they make one of metal?

R.B.: They have made bassoons of plastic, never of metal in the way they make clarinets and flutes. They have made plastic bassoons, but they have never been satisfactory. I haven't explained the form of the instrument. It's nine feet long, though it doesn't look it, because it's doubled on itself like a huge U and it's lined with ebony. You actually blow in about the middle of it. Now when you blow into an instrument, you get condensation—and this is not spit! You know, you see someone emptying out a horn or something and say, 'Oh, God, isn't that disgusting.' All it is is condensation, such as you get on the inside of a car window if the temperature drops.

A.S.: If you play an instrument like the bassoon I think you probably take it up because you want to play with other people. Is there a lot of music written for the bassoon?

R.B.: Yes, there is an immense amount. Vivaldi wrote no less than 39 bassoon concertos, which is a remarkable feat, and the bassoon was played very commonly then. And not only Vivaldi but other composers of that period wrote concertos and also chamber works which featured the bassoon: quartets with say violin, viola, cello and bassoon as a solo instrument. At the time of Beethoven, there was a composer no one's ever heard of except wind players, called Franz Danzi; he wrote an immense amount of work for wind instruments and it's very charming music, too. I think it was really during the nineteenth century that there was the sort of vogue for huge orchestras and the bassoon was considered very much as a part of the orchestra and they forgot that it did have these qualities as a solo instrument. Very sad. There are notable exceptions to that; Weber wrote a concerto and a Hungarian rondo for bassoon—although viola-players imagine it was written for them, but only because *they* have the same frustration over repertoire!

A.S.: How long have you been first bassoon with the L.S.O.?

R.B.: Almost exactly five years this Christmas. I think I'm right in saying I've played in all the London-based symphony orchestras with the exception of the B.B.C. Symphony. I also had four years playing in various Continental orchestras, which is another story. I've never been in any other orchestra more than three years and I think this is indicative somewhat, because I have enjoyed my time so much with the L.S.O. For various reasons; partly because one always has this terrific challenge and this standard to keep up, because I'm sitting in the middle of a wind section which has got really some of the finest instrumentalists I know anywhere in the world. And this I enjoy. You are not allowed to relax at all.

And this is what it's like, playing in London. It has these satisfactions but it's very difficult to do other things as well.

A.S.: Is it also the reason that you are not married?

R.B.: Playing in any big symphony orchestra in London does restrict one—particularly as I seem to have always had the misfortune to work in an orchestra which doesn't allow lady players! It is very difficult to meet people, actually; I was speaking to somebody the other day who gave up his job in one of the big London symphony orchestras for that very reason.

A.S.: Where did he go?

R.B.: He now plays in a chamber orchestra which he says is fine— 'All these lovely birds around. I've never met them before. I didn't even know they were there. I just imagined they must be and I've never looked back on the day I left the L.S.O.'—it was the L.S.O. actually.

A.S.: Don't you meet the public, though?—in the intervals in concerts some of them come backstage.

R.B.: It's jolly difficult. You have got all those sharks in the orchestra who pounce on anyone, you know, and I find it very very difficult to compete.

A.S.: I don't really believe that!

Roger Birnstingl was married on Saturday, 9th May.

PART FOUR

The Horns and Brass

IVAN DAVID GRAY

Principal Horn

A.S.: There are a lot of elements in the London Symphony Orchestra at the present time that are going American—for instance, we record for American companies, we play regularly in Carnegie Hall and this is the fourth year we are going to the Daytona Festival in Florida. We have an American Manager and Principal Conductor.

Although English, you have spent some time in America, haven't you, David?

D.G.: Yes, I was there for twelve years. I wasn't aware that the L.S.O. was being consciously Americanised, but it has recorded for American companies, mainly because the American companies occupy a very large proportion of the recording business. R.C.A. and C.B.S. are very large companies. Rather than say Americanise, I would prefer to say internationalise.

A.S.: Do you think this is a trend with symphony orchestras? Can you see us recording for, say, an Italian company?

D.G.: If an Italian company existed—I don't know of one offhand that would be financially capable of supporting an orchestra of the L.S.O. standard.

A.S.: In a sense the L.S.O. has always been outward looking from England. I am thinking of that American tour in 1912, when the orchestra was booked on the maiden voyage of the *Titanic*, cancelled out a few days before, and just missed the disaster.

D.G.: It does appear to have been historically a pioneering orchestra. The very idea of going to America then, which was pretty much of a backwoods country and very rough and ready, seems scarcely imaginable.

A.S.: Yes, knowing of the difficulties of organising a tour today, one wonders how they ever managed to arrange such a project in those times.

Do you like the self-governing arrangements in England? Do you think it is good artistically and financially?

D.G.: I think anything is a good arrangement if it works both artistically and financially. It appears to have worked for some period of time, although when one becomes involved in the structure of it—

as any member of a self-governing orchestra does, whether he wants to or not—one can see certain drawbacks in the system. It's the closest thing, perhaps, to the perfect democracy which is a sort of pie-in-the-sky thing anyway. There are things which just don't get done; one can become frustrated, particularly if they apply to what you happen to be doing—if I want something done in my section, or anything like that. I can see drawbacks in this way. On the other hand I can see advantages in that the individual has more identity.

A.S.: There are of course organisational problems which do affect the end result, but are there any harmful effects that bear directly on artistic standards in the self-governing system?

D.G.: I think that majority opinion is not necessarily always the right one.

A.S.: We are giving the impression that all the decisions are taken by all of the orchestra all of the time, and I think the disadvantages you have just described are, to some extent, met by having directors elected for three years only, so that there is a bit of stability for those three years. How do American orchestras compare to English ones?

D.G.: American orchestras are more disciplined. Now the elaboration of the word 'discipline' is, of course, endless; I really don't want to go into that too much, but the classic example would be if you go into a recording studio in which a London orchestra was to begin recording at—say two in the afternoon; you will probably find that at five minutes to two there may be about six people sitting down—and this is quite standard procedure—and as if by magic people start coming out of the walls about two minutes before the downbeat! On the other hand, an American orchestra will probably be there five or ten minutes before. It is a much more disciplined organisation and I think in that way can be more efficient.

A.S.: They haven't got that umbrella protection of their independent democracy in America, have they?

D.G.: They haven't. But the benefits written into their contracts are quite substantial!

A.S.: Now what about this comparison: do American orchestras play better than English ones, in general?

D.G.: Well, this is like saying: 'Which is the best orchestra in the world?'

A.S.: Well, which is?

D.G.: I don't think it is possible to equate orchestras in such a way.

A.S.: Talking then, not comparatively, but just about the L.S.O. as it is, would you like to say what you think its good qualities are, and also criticise it a bit?

D.G.: Somehow, in a way, the two things almost coincide. The good quality is the almost fantastic ability to pull things out of a top hat, in a situation in which there is very little rehearsal time, or the schedule is particularly tight. Really substantial concerts, fine concerts, perhaps great concerts, have occurred in my time with the orchestra in situations where you would think: 'This is going to be a disaster'.

At the same time this haphazardness, this kind of approach, doesn't always come off. Given the wrong conductor and the wrong situation, it can degenerate into something which I would consider not a worthwhile experience—to put it mildly—so that my praise and criticism really stem from the same thing.

A.S.: What are the main problems that confront you when playing first horn in a symphony orchestra?

D.G.: I think the main problem is coping with the tense atmosphere which prevails at concerts and recording sessions. That in itself produces problems which don't exist in more relaxed rehearsals.

A.S.: What makes the atmosphere in a recording studio tense?

D.G.: The fact that the orchestra and you are hired for a given amount of time which is strictly budgeted for; you are there to make a record in so many sessions and extra time is not usually possible—certainly rarely to accommodate the musicians. The recording has to be done to the best of your ability in the prescribed time. All sorts of funny things go wrong in a recording session—as has happened to me many times. In the middle of an important solo, somebody will drop something in the studio and we have to start again. Perhaps the second time through you crack a note. This of course means that that particular take is not useable. The third time round maybe somebody creaks a floor board or something. You are in a situation where you have to have a reserve to enable you to cope with a solo not just once, as in a concert, but perhaps six or seven times.

A.S.: How much of this reserve does a first class professional principal have—is it ever likely that you won't be able to deliver?

D.G.: If I weren't able to deliver, I wouldn't be doing what I am now! I only hope that I am able to spot my deficiencies before other people do.

A.S.: If you are tense and nervous what is the first thing that goes? Is it cracking notes?

D.G.: It's very hard to say. I think possibly from a wind player's point of view the most vulnerable thing is breath control, a slight quiver appears in the sound and so on . . . It's *normal* breathing control that's under stress, but somehow that seems to be the Achilles' heel of it all.

A.S.: When you were building up this reserve to enable you to cope with tense situations did you evolve any special processes of self-discipline to help you?

D.G.: No, not anything specific. There are systems which enable people to cope with these situations. The most obvious one is Yoga, which is used by quite a few musicians; it is a means of physical discipline which enables the mind to control aspects of tension and so on. . . .

A.S.: Have you used that?

D.G.: I haven't, no, but I've thought about it. It is a highly valid means of coping with situations like that. I think that people often don't understand the nature of the tension under which they work.

A.S.: Do these stresses only apply to principal players or do the others in the section suffer similarly?

D.G.: I would think everyone in the orchestra to a degree suffers from this; everyone in the orchestra is a responsible musician, bent on performing to the best of his ability.

A.S.: They put the pressure on themselves, really?

D.G.: The pressure is there, by the way we work, by what recording companies and conductors expect from us, or if you are honest with yourself as an individual or as a musician then there is tension involved in having to do your best all the time.

A.S.: Is there more tension in a symphony orchestra context than, say, chamber music or concerto playing?

D.G.: It's difficult to equate pressure. Chamber music is by its very nature more exposed, yet for me curiously it has a more relaxed atmosphere than playing in the orchestra. It's more taxing to play eight exposed bars in the orchestra than say the complete Schubert Octet, where many more notes are involved. More personally, there is much more communication with the players around you in chamber music —perhaps it's because an orchestra is slightly anonymous that you feel more exposed.

A.S.: Do you do much concerto playing?

D.G.: I haven't done any concerto playing at all; since Dennis Brain, England has had more than its fair share of horn concerto players. I've thought about doing it—obviously thinking about it doesn't produce any kind of result—but I don't consider the pieces written for solo horn to be that valid musically. The Mozart Horn Concertos are pleasant; the Strauss pieces are interesting, but only incidental Strauss. There is only one piece in the repertoire that I would consider musically valid in a symphonic sense and that is the Hindemith Concerto.

A.S.: You must have played by now with many different conductors. If you are the first horn you've got to take the initiative and be there, at some point on the beat, and if this varies with different conductors how do you know when to blow?

D.G.: Generally speaking, conductors will tell you if what you are doing is not what they have in mind, but not always. It is not every conductor's good luck to have the technical knowledge of all the instruments in the orchestra at his fingertips—you can nearly always spot a pianist conductor because he only reaches as far as the first row of woodwinds.

A.S.: Why is that peculiar to pianists?

D.G.: If the piano is his musical foundation, he is accustomed to producing sounds by pressing keys and achieving an instantaneous response; he is not usually well versed with the mechanics of drawing a bow across the string, breathing, forming an embouchure and producing a note which even then, in the case of the horn, has to negotiate twelve feet of tubing as a vibration before an actual sound comes out.

A.S.: So his cues might be given earlier or later if he did understand those things?

D.G.: I think so, yes. Once you understand the nature of different sound productions you accommodate for them unconsciously.

French horns conferring.

A.S.: How do you feel, sitting in the orchestra for a performance of Tchaikovsky's Fifth Symphony when you know you are going to have this very exposed solo in the Slow Movement—in an important concert: does that worry you, or are you relaxed about it?

D.G.: The feeling for that particular piece is one of extreme discomfort, but one learns to live through this. It's a very difficult thing not to make a complete hash of the First Movement simply anticipating the Second. It's true of all pieces, you have to pace yourself. A classic example of that kind of thing, a simple solo taken by itself, comes at the very end of the New World Symphony of Dvorak. You find yourself sitting there waiting for it, knowing that everyone else is waiting for it, too, and that to fluff it spoils the performance for everyone.

A.S.: It always seems to come off with us. . . .

D.G.: Well, I can think of a few times when it hasn't and I was very embarrassed!

A.S.: How old were you when you first met the French horn?

D.G.: I was fourteen—it was in High School in Pittsburgh.

A.S.: Can you remember how many years it was from that time to when you were first earning your living as a professional horn player?

D.G.: I went to the Curtis Institute in 1960 and the students there did quite a lot of freelance work in Philadelphia. They are very fortunate because Philadelphia has two opera companies, quite good ones, and there also are a lot of little orchestras around which draw quite heavily on students at Curtis, which is a very good school and people can rely on a certain standard. So I really started earning my living in my third year at Curtis which would be 1962.

A.S.: Or some eight years after you first started to learn the French horn. What is your own taste in music, not as a player, but just as a person?

D.G.: Well, I do identify with what I play; I think most people do. If one is fortunate enough to be a principal, it is quite sensible to listen to recordings, on which you happen to be playing something which is audible, and evaluating yourself. Listening is a bit of a busman's holiday most of the time. A very large percentage of my records are L.S.O. for that reason, and also because I'm interested in the orchestra. Aside from that, I have no sympathy at all with pop music. Perhaps it is enough as a musician just to be bombarded by the radio, but doing a few sessions as well really put the lid on the whole thing as far as I am concerned. Jazz is something which I have played, being in the States this is not surprising, and I have always enjoyed playing it and therefore I listen to it quite a lot.

A.S.: You mean you play jazz on the French horn? That's very unusual, isn't it?

D.G.: Unusual but not unique. There have been jazz horn players. Again, always American.

A.S.: Of course most people think of the horn as being one of the least articulate of instruments, in that the florid passages appear to be difficult. Surely in jazz you need to be very fluent, able to run about quite a bit at will—and freely, to extemporise? Is this why the horn has not become popular in general as a jazz instrument?

D.G.: I don't really buy this, because, if anything, the most difficult instrument on which to execute florid passages in jazz is the trombone. People have got round this. I think really it is a question of the horn being a valve instrument. It has a certain fluency by its very nature which a slide instrument hasn't. Most jazz players who have left a lasting impression are black; it could be that their environment doesn't happen somehow to encompass the French horn.

A.S.: It always occurs to me that if you are a musician and have a certain amateur ability on an instrument, you either can or can't play jazz easily. Do you agree with this or do you think it is something which can be taught?

D.G.: Taught, no. Very much not.

A.S.: Why is that?

D.G.: It's an enigma which I suppose we could go on talking about and really never solve for a long time. I think it must have something to do with basic feeling. When you are improvising you are thinking before you are playing. You haven't got any notes to read. When you are reading notes I believe most players see the note—there is some sort of physical linkage involved—so you read the note first and then you transpose it physically into what you have to do to produce it on the instrument—and out comes a note, with any luck. Improvising is like this except that it's done with regard to ideas. It is being able to translate an idea, or even maybe cook it up in the first place, into the physical terms which enable you to produce it on the instrument; and this is something which doesn't necessarily mean that because a person is a fan of jazz, and knows every recording from early 52nd Street Bop onwards, he can do it, no matter how accomplished a musician he may be.

A.S.: Now, coming down to the fundamental things about the horn, in terms of someone who might like the sounds it makes, and might like to try it, can you advise them how to go about this? How would you advise, say, a boy of fourteen who has heard the horn, or has just seen it, and would like to play it?

'Everyone in the orchestra is a
responsible musician, bent on performing
to the best of his ability.'
Ivan David Gray, horn.

D.G.: What I would say is that the most important thing is for some-one to become interested in the instrument by listening; that is an essential interest which can be carried on by, well, frankly, listening some more. My first experience of the horn sound was something like The Waltz of the Flowers—four horns in harmony—which has just that kind of super resonant sound which appeals to almost anybody. If any young person has become interested to that degree then I would say, go along to a library and get some records, and listen some more; and then get him to discover what there is in the town in the way of music education, and refer him to the nearest professional. Professional advice in any capacity as early as possible for any instrument is very important; and professionals are very kind in this respect; they are quite free with their advice.

A.S.: Does the French horn get better as it gets older, or should one really get a new one to start with?

D.G.: Well, not being made of wood and not having a sacred Italian name engraved on it, it doesn't do things like that.

A.S.: What about the symphony orchestra itself? Do you think there will always be a place for the sort of orchestra that we generally play in today; that is Beethoven's orchestra?

D.G.: The thing that alarms me most is to infer that orchestras will become museums; that the composers who wrote for these orchestras will become antiquated artistically. In other words, Mozart and Beethoven are to become museum pieces. If this is so, then I think it is a rather sad comment on the way society is progressing.

A.S.: The L.S.O. is one of the last major capital symphony orches-tras not to admit women.

D.G.: I can't see any immediate advantage to myself in there being any, artistically or otherwise. It is the only one that doesn't admit women. I don't hold a strong position about this, as some members do. Some are particularly vociferous about this and against it. I think I would prefer to be practical about it, in that, if it were a question of not having a player who was obviously superior to another candidate for a position who happened to be a woman, then it would be artistic nonsense to turn her down. There are other arguments about this which could be gone into. Things like touring, in which different people have different problems, and men and women under certain duress and strain respond in different ways.

I never think of the L.S.O. as being special because there are no women in it. There are so many forms of prejudice in the world, and that is one of the older ones, which most people seem to have got rid of or talked their way around. There are others which concern people more than that now.

A.S.: It is a well known fact that the L.S.O. works very hard, that six to nine hours a day is not unusual, and often seven days a week. Do you have enough time when you are not working to have interesting, varied activities apart from music?

D.G.: If I am frustrated, I can't trace it to any lack of activities outside music. How's that for skating around the question?

HOWARD SNELL
Principal Trumpet

A.S.: Say how you first came to take up the trumpet.

H.S.: I learned to play the cornet at a very early age—the cornet is very close to the trumpet, but is usually more available and is slightly easier to play, so it's a handy introduction to trumpet-playing—and my father, being a good musician, insisted that I knew the basic rudiments first. At school I never had any doubt that what I wanted in adult life was to be a musician. Three years were spent at the Academy—really of very little interest from a music education point of view, because our academies of music are very badly organised for the orchestral musician. In 1960 I was invited to join the L.S.O. as third trumpet, Alan Stringer being appointed principal trumpet from Liverpool at the same time. I remained as third trumpet for a short while, then was assistant principal and finally was appointed to the full co-principal position in 1967. This is one of the most difficult jobs in the profession in that it means playing first constantly and, in the L.S.O., trying to play to the highest standards.

A.S.: Of course if one goes to a concert one is aware of the first trumpet all the time. It must be a big responsibility with a great orchestra to keep up the standard?

H.S.: You can never hide what you do because of the prominence of the trumpet's tone, unlike say a horn or a woodwind instrument; it is impossible to hide the sound you make under the resonance and the timbres of other instruments. Many things affect you when you are playing; the temperature of the hall can make one's embouchure puffy and sweaty, which has an effect on embouchure calculations; and if it's cold it is difficult to make one's musculature work properly.

A.S.: It was rather hot and sweaty, I thought, in the concert we have just finished. Did this affect you tonight?

H.S.: No, it wasn't too bad tonight because even though the temperature was high there was continual ventilation. The problem of stamina is an ever present one, apart from all the problems of playing with other people satisfactorily and interpreting the visual hieroglyphics that conductors like to throw at you.

A.S.: You have to know the different hieroglyphic vocabulary of each conductor, do you?

H.S.: Yes, it's necessary. The difficulty with a trumpet is that, being such a direct kind of instrument, you have always to be very sure of your attack, and it is almost impossible to slide in unseen and produce a kind of nice average entry in terms of precision.

A.S.: Now you always seem to me—in fact most trumpet players do —to be pretty cool, calm and collected. But I'm sure that's just a front. If you go on to a platform and you feel unsure of yourself, if there hasn't been enough rehearsal, or if you don't like the conductor, how do you cope with feelings of nervousness or panic? How do you pull yourself round?

H.S.: I think very rarely is one bothered about conductors in the performance except in the case of technical incompetence on his part. Feelings of panic and nervousness are very difficult to control. One can feel nervous in a church hall, in the middle of nowhere, while one can feel completely calm on the stage of the most important places. Playing in Philadelphia last night, for instance, for some reason was of no consequence to me at all in terms of nerves, and yet one was playing in the home of one of the world's greater orchestras. We were very lucky, of course, in the concert in that it was very well received. I have been given to understand that a German team of psychologists studied orchestral players throughout Germany and discovered that, of all the positions in the orchestra, that of first trumpet entailed the most psychological stress—obviously for the reasons I have mentioned, the directness of the instrument and the fact that in no way can it be hidden. If you make a mistake, everybody knows.

A.S.: Well, what then is the fun in being the first trumpet?

H.S.: It's a job which tests you in terms of skill and professionalism. One learns techniques to deal with things like being nervous or having an off day. One can sense as soon as one gets up in the morning whether one is physically in good shape to play. If I feel off, then I must be very careful to warm up before the rehearsal or before the concert very very carefully so that I can induce all the right responses in the musculature and the breathing and so on.

A.S.: I was thinking more in terms of your general psychology and mood, walking onto the platform.

H.S.: One must be technically happy—one must go onto the platform and think that now with a modicum of luck everything will go well because I am technically in command of all the things that I am required to play this evening and therefore I can feel free to play as I want to musically. This is the key point. For instance, one learns that the nervous system has predictable ways of going wrong. One's breathing tightens up, one's chest and back tighten up; one can simply relax them by carefully relaxing one's arms, doing breathing exercises and being sure to be very well prepared. One simply learns foresight from mistakes of the past. Once you know that you can control your nerves and that to a reasonable extent you have prepared your embouchure and prepared your general playing feeling, then you trust yourself to the lap of the gods.

A.S.: There are no special rewards in this specially difficult seat?

H.S.: The special rewards are that if you do something difficult well, then one's sense of having done it is reward in itself; there really is very little to match it. In all one's experiences, throughout all kinds of things that one enjoys in one's private and public life, there is very little to match playing well. And there is very little as terrible and horrible to put up with as playing badly. This is it—playing badly and playing well are the two opposite extremes in my life.

A.S.: You were, I suppose, fortunate, weren't you, in being allowed to start the cornet at four years of age. Would you say this is the ideal age?

H.S.: No, this is not the ideal age. The trumpet is best started when the child is physically more fully formed than at the age of four. I still retain many embouchure defects because of starting early and not being adequately taught. If I had started later my faults would have grown up with me less—I would have been more independent physically of the instrument.

A.S.: For somebody who is musical at eight or nine or more and who wants to learn the trumpet, should they start on a cornet first?

H.S.: No, most trumpet players in the symphony orchestras of course did start on the cornet, but this is a reflection on the fact that the brass band movement in this country has always been very strong— less so now than previously. I would not start a child on the cornet unless it was going to stay in a brass band. A child should start on the instrument, on the kind of mouthpiece on which he means to continue later on, so as to be acquainted with the instrument which they are going to play on all their life, particularly the mouthpiece; during the formative years this is very very valuable. If a young child starts with a good teacher, then this is worth a great deal of musical ability which untaught, or badly taught, would be a struggle to patch up.

A.S.: How much does a reasonable trumpet cost?

H.S.: You might get one of the better makes second-hand for £50.

A.S.: What are the better makes?

H.S.: The better makes are generally all American makes: Vincent Bach, the Benge trumpet.

A.S.: I remember the story of a famous English trumpet player who was so proud of his specially designed mouthpiece that he would lay a handkerchief over it when he wasn't blowing so that the other trumpet players couldn't copy it. Do you have any particular views about design of trumpet mouthpieces?

H.S.: The mouthpiece I use is a very, very battered and rough Viennese mouthpiece—rather an old-fashioned style. In fact my mouthpiece is very badly made because the hole through the mouthpiece is not a perfect circle. It must have been very loose on the lathe when it was made!

A.S.: But you like it. . . .

H.S.: But I like it.

A.S.: What do you think of your lot as a professional trumpet player in an international orchestra? Is it much of a life? You've described all the difficulties—nervous tension, responsibility and the work that must constantly go into maintaining the standard. What sort of a life is it?

H.S.: It's a very very good life. I do something which I enjoy because I can test my skill to its utmost and do well. This means one can do equally badly; the tension of trying to do well when it succeeds is so much the more rewarding. I never thought seriously of ever doing anything else.

A.S.: How important is music generally to you?

H.S.: Honestly that sort of question never occurs to me. In my childhood I played a great deal on the piano and still do, although now I'm more enthusiastic than proficient. During my latter school days I played the piano more than I did the cornet. Now the piano repertoire is a wonderful hobby.

A.S.: For the past two years you have been one of the nine elected directors of the London Symphony Orchestra—so as well as knowing the orchestra from the concert platform out, you have known it from 1 Montague Street out as well. What do you think of the self-governing system with which the L.S.O. has really taken the lead in London? We were the first orchestra to have this system in 1904, and have been imitated perhaps by three other orchestras since. Do you think there are advantages? And do you think there are any disadvantages?

H.S.: I've been in the L.S.O. for ten years and behind the changes in management and changes in chief conductor—the kind of thing which serves to make up newspaper articles—the L.S.O. itself has quite consistently and steadily improved. Even critics and other people who at one time were very pleased to make a great fuss of the L.S.O. as the new darling of the orchestral world are a little tired of this now; but the quality of the L.S.O. is better now than it has ever been at any time since I've been in the orchestra. Obviously the problems facing us are very large—the problems of how to keep good players in the orchestra, to prevent them from leaving to freelance in the very green pastures of the freelance world. But possibly the greatest problem we have is the shortage of great conductors. It may be an illusion to think that the general standard of conductors these days is lower than it has been formerly, but using one's rule-of-thumb judgment I would point this out as the greatest difficulty; and orchestras more and more must come to depend on themselves as their own arbiters of standards and their own disciplinarians.

A.S.: Do the player directors of the orchestra have any real control at all over what happens? Isn't it the manager, the musical hierarchy in London that really make the decisions? Do you feel that you have an effective voice?

H.S.: The managers and the hierarchy have an influence, as we all have our different abilities to emphasise. I think of it as a working-together rather than a conflict. Of course, there is a certain amount of unofficial pushing and shoving. London enjoys quantity and quality as no other city does, and the fulcrum of this situation is the orchestras. Getting back to the L.S.O., I certainly feel that the Board of Directors operates at quite a high level of efficiency; in programme planning, finance, the simple everyday commercial management of the orchestra, we are well organised. This of course is in co-operation with the other interested parties like the Arts Council. But still essentially control of the L.S.O. is in the hands of the member directors.

A.S.: But have players, talented musicians, really got the overall culture and intelligence to direct a really mammoth operation of the size of a major symphony orchestra?

H.S.: It is impossible to play a musical instrument to the standard we require in the L.S.O. without having intelligence to a very real degree, practical and theoretical. One point seems to me exceptionally noteworthy, if one has in mind that success is often cyclic, even in those businesses most subject to the minute calculation and the slide rule, that we survived a period of great difficulty—musical as well as commercial—a few years ago when the momentum of the first success cycle was slackening. This orchestra is now entirely superior to the orchestra then. Another idea is that of the worker controlling his own work: in the orchestras of London, particularly the L.S.O., the originator of 'player control', this idea has been fulfilled successfully. If we wanted to please everyone we could call it a 'free enterprise co-operative'!—which must be galling for the non-playing captains of music!

The success of the L.S.O. in becoming one of the world's leading orchestras—this is something said by other people and not by us; its success commercially in the recording field and its concert success— the activity most important to us; its success in every field except that of financial riches—all this is testimony to the success of player control.

DENIS WICK

Principal Trombone

A.S.: For how many years have you been with the London Symphony Orchestra?

D.W.: I joined the orchestra in 1957. I had been embedded in the Birmingham Symphony Orchestra for something approaching five years, and quite suddenly there came opportunities to do auditions. I eventually did an audition for the London Symphony Orchestra and decided to choose the L.S.O. rather than the other things.

A.S.: Why did you choose the L.S.O.?

D.W.: I don't know really, because at that time the L.S.O. wasn't in the favoured position that it has been in since.

The first concert I did when I joined the L.S.O. in April 1957 was a Tchaikovsky concert with the 1812 and the B Flat Minor Piano Concerto—and that sort of thing went on for several years; it really began to emerge that it was a good orchestra in 1957, with concerts with Stokowski and Dorati, and gradually over the years since then it has consistently improved, although one doesn't like to blow one's own trumpet—or should I say trombone—about one's own orchestra.

A.S.: I think that people are jealous of the standard of playing. I know that if we have one player in the orchestra who is obviously not good enough, about a dozen people immediately come in a very subtle way and make sure that you realise it, if you are on the personnel committee. That sort of thing keeps up the standard.

D.W.: Nowadays also we tend not to make mistakes, because there are enough good players in the orchestra to allow very careful choosing of new people, and the general standard is rising all the time. We have more to offer in the way of prestige than we had twelve or fourteen years ago.

A.S.: What are the special difficulties of playing the trombone? The mouthpiece is much bigger than the trumpet.

D.W.: Yes, that is true. In some ways it is easier to start playing the trombone than the other brass instruments, but it sorts out the sheep from the goats in that if you don't have a really good sense of co-ordination—a good ear and the necessary moral fibre or stamina to put in a great deal of very boring practice—it is pretty well impossible. I think most brass instruments are easy to start with; that is why amateur bands have flourished, either purely brass or brass and wind. But even in America where there are 52,000 school bands, there is still no more than a handful, comparatively speaking, of really top notch trombone players, and this has always surprised me. I think the special difficulties with the trombone are to do with musicianship more than anything else.

A.S.: What about the sheer physical size of it? It must take a lot of wind?

D.W.: It doesn't need any more wind than is needed to vibrate the air within the instrument.

A.S.: How long is the tubing on the trombone?

D.W.: The basic tubing is nine feet—fully extended that can add about another five which makes a total of fourteen feet. Sometimes, of course, we have trombones with extra tubing at the back of them which can be let in by pressing a lever on a rotary valve; this adds another four or five feet. This is how the bass trombone works in particular, because by combining all the lengths of tubes it helps to play some of the lower notes.

A.S.: That is a lot of air to move though: when you start playing the trombone a lot does it affect you physically?

D.W.: I think it was Charles Burney—in the seventeenth century— who said that the study of the bass trombone particularly was conducive to good health—it certainly makes you breathe properly which very few people ever do. You *have* to breathe fairly efficiently or you just can't to anything at all; it is certainly better for you to breathe more deeply, to get more oxygen going into the body. I know some brass players who have had very long and very healthy lives into their eighties and nineties. But to play Wagner or a Bruckner symphony leaves one feeling very tired and I think physically tired at that. You couldn't play as many notes as a string player because you would be physically incapable of doing so.

A.S.: What about the business of not having valves on the instrument. Is it much more difficult to find the notes without valves?

D.W.: The difficulties are really similar because you have to select tube length, either by depressing valves or by moving the slide into the required position, and then make the lips buzz at the right frequency in order to give the sound. Moving the slide is a more cumbersome procedure, that's all. Adolph Sax, who was also responsible for the saxophone, did much to adopt piston valves into old and new brass instruments. He didn't invent the valve system, but he was in a very influential political situation in nineteenth-century France and more or less introduced the saxophone, the saxhorn, the cornet, a piston and all the various tubas and so on that arrived at about that time. He was politically influential in the French Army and caused all kinds of instruments that were otherwise used in French Army bands to be discontinued—so that his inventions could take their place. One of the things he tried to do was to introduce valve trombones, but fortunately various similarly influential people insisted on keeping the slide trombone—Berlioz was one of these people. It never actually disappeared. Of course, the intonation difficulties with three valves are pretty enormous, but the great thing about the slide trombone is that you are, theoretically at least, capable of playing every note perfectly in tune. The saying that there are no out of tune trombones, only out of tune trombone-players, has a certain validity. But although you are capable of playing them in tune you are also equally capable of playing them out of tune!

A.S.: Although the trombone glissando is a characteristic feature.

D.W.: Oh yes, this glissando of the trombone is the thing that distinguishes it from all the others; but of course people perhaps don't realise that all the string instruments can make glissandos, too.

A.S.: What is the modern trombone as used in the orchestra today? Is it American?

D.W.: Yes, it is a curious thing but we use American instruments more or less exclusively, and we don't make exactly the same sound on them as Americans do, which is again rather strange. People say that we make a German sound on American instruments. Some conductors like a particular type of sound quality. Dorati likes, for instance, a very brash, hard sound. If you play for German conductors they generally like a mellow sound with not quite such a degree of fortissimo. One of the ways that we have accomplished this particular sound that we make on American instruments is by very careful selection of mouthpieces. I have got round it in a slightly different way by designing my own mouthpiece—which I now sell and I have made a little business out of. They have gone extremely well and surprisingly enough they sell very well in America.

A.S.: What about British made instruments?

D.W.: British-made instruments used to be very good when there was a multiplicity of competitive British firms who made them, but they have suffered a kind of decline, mainly because British firms have been selling to more or less undiscriminating markets—the Zulu Police Band and the Turkish Navy, for instance. You can be pretty sure this will reflect on their instruments. The professional players to whom they should be supplying instruments generally buy American.

I have always been a bit concerned about this and have from time to time spoken to people at Boosey and Hawkes, who are the best instrument makers, to ask why on earth they don't make instruments that are good enough for us to use. I think we have now convinced them, and in fact the last assault I tried with Boosey and Hawkes seems to have worked.   We had half a dozen trombone players down there playing different instruments, with each of us giving detailed criticisms of them. This I think has resulted in a realization of our needs; they have now decided to introduce a completely new range of instruments —starting off with a symphony model which I have instigated. We are carrying out the first field tests next week. This has taken a year from when it was first started.

We hope it will be something like half the price of the American instruments. The British prices of American instruments are inflated very heavily with duty and purchase tax.

A.S.: What is it going to cost the student to buy a good trombone?

D.W.: Well, hopefully, to buy the Boosey and Hawkes instruments that I have been involved with, I would think something like £100 or maybe slightly less.

A.S.: When did you first start to play the instrument?

D.W.: When I was about ten years old. My father was the local band secretary, and this was really fascinating to me.

A.S.: Well, did you pick up a trombone one day and think this was for you?

D.W.: I think I had one put into my hand and everybody stood around to see what would happen; so I made a noise on it and it all started then. My father gave me my first lessons.

A.S.: Was your father a musician?

D.W.: Oh yes, he played the old fashioned G bass trombone— the extraordinary thing with a handle on it—and also the tuba, or bass as it is called in the brass band. I think every bandsman wants to see his son play, and every son wants to do what his father did or does. In the same way my own son has become a tuba player, having started to play the trombone a little.

A.S.: Is he going to be a professional tuba player?

D.W.: I think he would like to be one, although I have rather advised him against it in the way that many professional players do.

A.S.: Why, in your case?

D.W.: I have often asked myself this. *I* certainly wouldn't do any-thing else, except perhaps run a business—which I think I could prob-ably do, having seen a great deal of inefficiency in all directions whenever I have looked at business. But I think that Stephen is gifted in other directions and he has a good enough brain to do many other equally rewarding things—and I think there is still this feeling of insecurity about the musical profession. We still have this now.

'There is so much to enjoy in music.' ▶
Denis Wick, trombone.

A.S.: Yes, but in London, although there is no security, most of the musicians do quite well.

D.W.: I just wonder how much this is an artificial situation. If, for instance, the B.B.C. ceased to do any more broadcasting of live music apart from using their own staff orchestras—this is on the face of it inconceivable, but it could just happen; if there were no more film recordings because of a depression in that particular field; if gramo-phone recording were stopped for a similar reason; if, in fact, there were any kind of economic depression, I think musicians would be the first people to suffer.

A.S.: The L.S.O. works pretty full time, but the trombones aren't used all the time; what other activities do you have?

D.W.: The Guildhall School is fairly time consuming. I have fourteen students there of varying standards. I share the direction of the Guildhall Concert Band—this is a development of the old-fashioned military band that one used to hear in every seaside town and is intended to make a sound nearer to a symphony orchestra than a band.

A.S.: And what else do you do?

D.W.: Well there is the mouthpiece thing; I spend a lot of time messing around with the mouthpieces until they come out right.

A.S.: What about films and commercial sessions—do you do any of that?

D.W.: Oh yes, but this is something that you can't depend on really. I have the usual sort of fleeting contacts with 'fixers' who will take somebody like me from a symphony orchestra more or less in despera-tion because their regular people who are normally more likely to be free can't do the work. I may then be booked for a couple of days' films.

A.S.: What about chamber music? Is there a place for trombones?

D.W.: I have wanted for a long time to run a quartet of trombones, choosing people whose playing I like particularly, and even to some extent using people who have studied with me, because we all tend to play in the same sort of way these days.

A.S.: What about solo work on the trombone? I remember you playing a concerto written for you by Gordon Jacob.

D.W.: There are, I suppose, half a dozen or so concertos worth playing. The difficulty with solo work on the trombone is that nobody wants to hear you—mainly because they haven't any idea of the enormous range of dynamics, or style, of things that the instrument can do when it is unshackled from the orchestra. It is something like having a sports car towing a very big caravan; when you release the caravan you can do all kinds of things that most listeners would not think possible.

A.S.: What composers do you like playing most with the orchestra?

D.W.: Those that write best for the instrument I suppose. I really enjoy, for instance, playing the high Mozart parts on the alto trombone in the Requiem Mass, the Vespers. It is delightful to play in a small orchestra and not to have to play loudly and be a fill-in, but to be playing almost like a woodwind instrument, although one is in fact doubling choral parts most of the time. I think that the composer I like least is Beethoven because the parts are generally not particularly interesting and at the same time extremely hard; the first trombone part is for alto trombone and is hard to play because I am not so very accustomed to playing on the alto instrument—and it is very high to play on the tenor trombone. I really enjoy playing Wagner, Strauss, Mahler—because it is so well written—and Sibelius—because one puts so much into the atmosphere. Strangely enough, I rather enjoy playing Schubert and I think every trombone player would agree with that because so much of his music for the trombone is used more in a wood-wind context. The general concert audience public—and many orchestral players—regard the trombone as being something of a noise maker, because this is the function that we unfortunately have to perform most of the time. I am sure viola players, for instance, don't like having to scrub tremolo chords fortissimo for hours on end—the sort of thing you do in film studios—and a lot of the stuff that we have to do comes into that category.

A.S.: And more modern composers?

D.W.: Well, I think most orchestral players haven't much regard for the most modern composers—the people who expect you to make noises that you haven't ever thought of making before, although I don't subscribe to the view that there haven't been any good composers since Richard Strauss. I view with a little less than tolerance the out-pourings of people like Berio, for instance—the modern composers who I think have very little in actual content to say. I can't help feeling that gimmickry comes into this more than it should. I think that all modern composers should start off by writing string quartets and stick to that for ten years.

A.S.: Do you like Britten?

D.W.: Oh yes, but I can't really regard Britten as being a modern composer in the same sense. I think Britten's work is so skilled and so well contrived—from the instrumentalist's point of view it is extremely well written. I suppose Schoenberg is an interesting composer to talk about as far as the trombone is concerned, because he was a great innovator. Without too much knowledge of the instrument, he tried to work things that he had in his mind and by very careful organis-ation of technique it is possible to play them, for instance, in the Five Orchestral Pieces or Moses and Aaron, there are extremely difficult things that you just *can* play and they are very effective.

'One can sense as soon as one gets
up in the morning whether one is
physically in good shape to play.'
Howard Snell, trumpet.

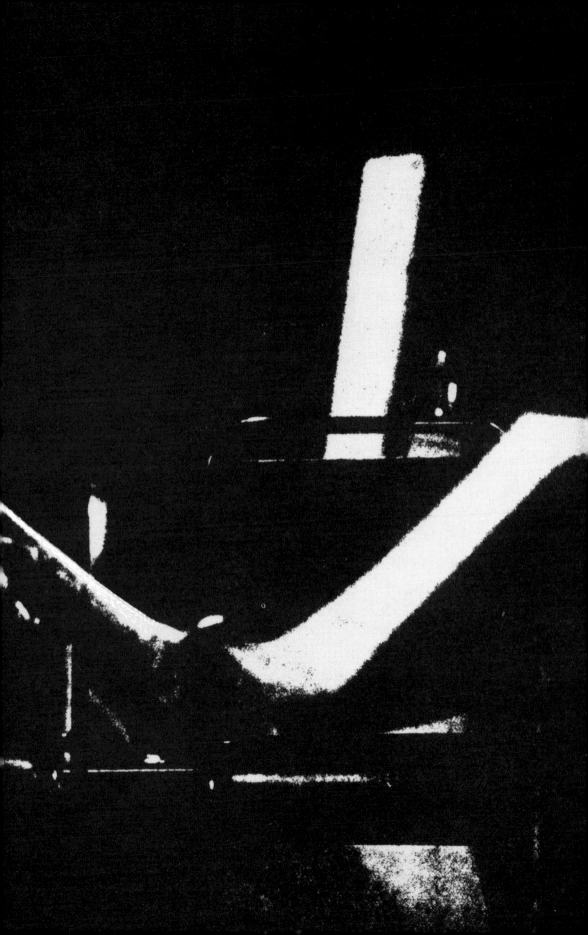

A.S.: Which composer though means more to you than any other, as a listener?

D.W.: I think Bach more than anyone really, but this has nothing to do with playing functions of course. It is just that for me I think the music of Bach is timeless; it says very simply so many things that so many people have since said so many more times but in a more roundabout kind of way. I strongly believe music to be a form of communication very akin to speech and although one cannot define in words what is being said in music one can understand it. Music can be understood in musical terms and, without being too precious about this, I think that this is the level on which most musicians listen to music. You are actually in communication with some-body long dead who is saying what he believes to be truths which you can understand, in the same way, without having to translate them into more mundane words.

A.S.: How important as a member of the L.S.O. is your indepen-dence—as an orchestra, I mean. There are some signs that the inde-pendence might be eroded.

D.W.: I would take it a stage further; I think the most important thing is my independence as an individual and although I am happy to be a member of the orchestra I would hate to sell myself body and soul to it, or to any other organisation. Perhaps I will regret saying this one day, but I regard the most important thing as being the commodity I sell, which is the sound that I make, the way that I play; I regard myself as selling this, via the L.S.O. if you like, to the public.

A.S.: Do you feel you have much say in the running of the orchestra?

D.W.: I would like to think that my views on the orchestra are shared by many people, not because they are *my* views, but because they are reasonably intelligent views which most people, after a fair amount of experience in the profession, arrive at. If there is anything which is obviously very bad, either in a player who is a possible new member, a conductor whose qualities one has overestimated, or any such thing, I say my piece. I am not afraid to say it because I regard myself as among friends.

A.S.: When you have finished with the orchestra, and with the mouthpieces, and with your instruments and doing the sessions, is there time for anything else? Do you collect stamps?

D.W.: No, I don't collect stamps! I spend quite a lot of time with the children when I can. I do a lot of driving. I suppose lots of music-ians, and I must be one of them, are in the rather happy position of enjoying what they do so much that it embodies bread and butter and jam, if you like, so that one is working at one's hobby—an ideal situation. I like to do decorating and painting and alterations—wood panels on walls and the sorts of things that most people do. Partly because I think I do it rather well—but again I try to carry it out in the same way as I do anything else, that if I do it I may as well make a decent job of it. I don't want walls cracking, I don't want panelling falling down.

A.S.: Yes, I get the impression that it is the playing that is important to you—you are non-political, and playing is all your life and all your interest, to an extraordinary extent, really.

D.W.: People say that I am a lunatic, a fanatic, but I think that it is only through devoting 95% of my energy to playing that I have managed to do what I have so far. I feel that I like to enjoy music on a completely different plane and forget about playing; this is very hard and in the long term I think this is one of the biggest sacrifices that a professional musician has to make, because he finds it virtually impossible to listen to music without relating it to his playing life. There is so much to enjoy in music that it can so easily be clouded by thinking of the way so and so is playing, and the way a particular conductor is conducting. One loses this enjoyment. I don't think the public realises what a big musical sacrifice a musician makes.

FRANK MATHISON

Bass Trombone

The trombone section of the modern symphony orchestra usually comprises three instruments: the first trombone, the second trombone and a third instrument, which is lower in pitch and bigger in size; this, the bass trombone, is played in the London Symphony Orchestra by Frank Mathison.

A.S.: What have your impressions been of eight years with the L.S.O.? I suppose the highlights have been the two world tours, have they?

F.M.: First of all, when I joined I thought it was absolutely great. You know, there was never anything out of place; we'd do concerts and you felt you dared not play something not together. It is not like that now. I think that when I joined the L.S.O. at first—I don't put all the blame on myself—but when I joined at first I thought it was absolutely fantastic and I am sure it is still the best orchestra. Sometimes the playing is absolutely fantastic, sometimes it is ordinary, but it never falls below a certain level and this is what has impressed me. Even on a schools' concert, there is still a high standard, which you don't get in a provincial orchestra.

A.S.: You work much harder in the L.S.O. than in a provincial orchestra, where you are on a salary, don't you?

F.M.: Work harder in the L.S.O.?—Well, you have more travelling to and from your place of work in the L.S.O.; from where I live in Harrow I waste a lot of time getting in and moving from the rehearsal place to a session.

A.S.: And we don't have any days off at all for several weeks running at a time.

F.M.: Well, the trombones do.

A.S.: Because you are not in all the pieces?

F.M.: I suppose we are in most concerts: in recording sessions, we may do a patch of Mozart, Beethoven and things—we are only in two of the Beethoven Symphonies, the Fifth and Ninth, and the tenor trombones are in the Sixth—but it is very easy for us to have a thin time. I am always earning such a lot more than I ever earned in the Birmingham orchestra, but I'm never better off.

A.S.: Do you have plenty of time for other interests?

F.M.: Well, my big interest, up to this year, was sailing—as you probably know—racing on the Welsh Harp. If I had a rehearsal in the morning, then I used to go racing in the afternoon and be back at the concert in the evening. Well, I must be getting old because I can't do that successfully now! And I need to rest a little bit.

A.S.: What is this other interest you have?—I remember you brought some blind children to one of our concerts and we went round and spoke to them in the interval.

F.M.: Yes, I've got a blind school band; I teach blind children to play brass instruments. It is in Wimbledon, which is quite a long way to go, and it needs a bit of time—in fact, I am getting a bit concerned now because I have a programme of Christmas Carols that I want to teach them and I am having trouble fitting it in. I have just lost a few players; I had a beautiful tuba player—he was playing absolutely marvellously and he had a wonderful memory; he could play in time and I really slogged at it because a tuba bass in a brass group is so essential. Being blind, they can't follow a beat, and so I was rather pleased with this boy managing it—and now he has passed his exams and gone on to Worcester. At the same time I have lost a girl playing a horn, and this happens all the time.

A.S.: How do you set about teaching them the parts, even of a carol—a reasonably simple little harmony like that?

F.M.: It depends on the child; you can't have a set way for any particular case. First of all I teach them the basics of the instrument and then I sing them the parts. They soon pick up the tune, but for the inner part you sing them whatever it happens to be and get them to play a little phrase so that they can memorise it—until they think their part is the tune. When you put it all together, of course, it sounds marvellous. I have got a tape at home of them playing. I composed a march for them which they were absolutely delighted with. I called it the Linden Lodge March—the school is the Linden Lodge School— and we gave a first performance at a concert. Since then we've tried to record it, but I've lost players and it is not as good as it was; I wish I'd got a recording of the first time they played it.

Very few children can understand braille music; they have got to be super-intelligent, I think. To read braille is one thing, but braille music is so much more complicated that, by the time they have learned a piece from braille music, they would have remembered it anyway.

A.S.: How did you come to be involved with this in the first place?

F.M.: I started in Birmingham—with the Blind School there. Harold Greensmith used to do it for them and when he died they got in touch with me. I suppose I was his star pupil and they wanted me to take over. When I came to London, I decided I was finished with teaching altogether, and then the Wimbledon school rang me up and said: 'We understand you ran the Blind School of Music in Birmingham—would you like to start a blind school here?'—And I thought I might as well.

A.S.: I must say I enjoyed meeting them that time. Will they come to anything else?

F.M.: Yes, I'm sure they will. They came that time because I had taken them to the L.S.O. Club and they had given a concert there; in return, the L.S.O. Club invited them to one of our concerts. It would be very nice for them to come again, but it is always a bit of trouble getting a coach and getting them organised to come to a concert.

A.S.: What is your opinion of the running of the L.S.O. as it now is? Have you got any strong criticisms of the system?

F.M.: I think, if you are well in with the people who are running it, it is a good idea: if you are not, it's not.

A.S.: You mean the Board?

F.M.: Yes, for some people . . . . you know, if they have got their own particular cronies on the Board, it can be very pleasant, I am sure, and it seems like a good way to run things. At one time, during the Barry Tuckwell regime, I was quite happy; I thought the Board was doing very well and was very good. People used to moan like hell about it, but I couldn't see what they were moaning about. I thought they were doing a good job, but when the situation had changed, and the Board had changed, I began to understand that you can never suit everybody!

A.S.: Well, I think the self-governing system, although cumbersome, does offer safeguards. You miss opportunities, because at times you move too slowly, but you make fewer mistakes.

F.M.: Perhaps I am being a bit vague about it. You have got the safeguard with the Board that there has to be a majority decision to get rid of someone.

A.S.: I think actually, since I've been on the Board, nobody has either been got rid of or sacked and I think if anything was going to happen like that it would almost certainly have to be unanimous. I don't think people would be very happy about taking such a drastic step unless it was exceptional. But at the moment, the main concern of the Board is not to make the mistake of getting the wrong people *into* the orchestra.

F.M.: Because once they are in you want to keep them in. The policy is not to sack people.

A.S.: Although you might have a chance of improving one seat—you can create a horrible atmosphere for everyone who is left, including yourself if you are running it. It is cumbersome, but I think it is marvellous that it works; and it must work, because we have been going for sixty-six years and all the other orchestras have copied us!

F.M.: There is no doubt about its working. You asked me my opinion of it, and I cannot say 'Yes, it is the only way'. But I think it is good; I can't think of a better system.

A.S.: But you imply that you are not as happy now as you were.

F.M.: Oh, I am quite happy in the orchestra now.

A.S.: What about conductors?—What about our principal conductor, Andre Previn, what do you think of him?

F.M.: I'll be absolutely honest about Previn. I like Previn. I think he is a terrific musician, I think he is a terrific pianist and I think playing at the piano and conducting the orchestra he is marvellous. I think the audience likes him and, from a business point of view, terrific. He has got a marvellous wit and personality with the orchestra—but he doesn't turn me on at all.

JOHN FLETCHER
Tuba

A.S.: The tuba is the bass instrument at the bottom of the brass choir; how did you come to play the tuba, John?

J.F.: My father was the music master at the school I attended—Leeds Modern School—and because of this we had a lot of instruments lying around at home. I used to pick them up and blow some of them, including a very good tuba which had been bequeathed to my father by someone. While I was at University, I took up the horn and then, in about my second year at University, doing science, I suddenly got very frustrated at the thought of being an amateur musician for the rest of my life—never playing with a better orchestra than the university one. And, I thought, when I left it would be very much worse; I decided then that I wanted to join an orchestra. It was a toss-up between the horn and the tuba. My idea was that if I couldn't be an absolutely first class horn—of the Tuckwell or Civil standard, I wouldn't bother. I didn't want to be a third horn and I would much rather be *the* tuba in an orchestra. It can be a very, very frustrating instrument, simply because there isn't a great deal to do, but I enjoy it; for myself I demand the right to sit around while other people are playing just to observe.

A.S.: That isn't really true, is it? The tuba is actually a very expressive, rather sweet sort of instrument.

J.F.: Oh yes, I am talking about basic minimum standards; the notes as they are set out in the score appear to most people to be rather uninteresting—but it depends how you approach these few notes. There are often very many more than just a few notes.

A.S.: But, like the double bass, you have a terrific influence in the brass choir?

J.F.: Yes, except that there again, as a double bass you are one of eight and if you drop out, nobody knows; but for most of the time you are the one and only tuba and if you drop out, well certainly everybody around you knows.

A.S.: In brass tuning are you extra specially responsible for intonation, being fundamental in most chords?

J.F.: Yes, I am excruciatingly conscious of this. It is one of the reasons why I joined the London Symphony Orchestra—because of Stuart Knussen; the trouble is that most bass sections have eight players bumbling on in their own way and the L.S.O. is the only orchestra that has succeeded in doing anything rather more than this.

A.S.: Why were you especially conscious of the bass section? Most people take it for granted.

J.F.: Most people don't hear them. I just happen to have an ear which is responsive to bass notes.

A.S.: And you can also hear high up—have you perhaps got an extended range of hearing?

J.F.: Well, actually I'm rather deaf.

A.S.: Are you really?

J.F.: A little bit deaf: industrial deafness.

A.S.: What's industrial deafness?

J.F.: Well, making a loud noise without at the same time being affected by it. I am at the same time very very sensitive indeed to noise —noise as defined by the International Physics Association in 1957. They met for a week and had learned discussions; then they defined a noise as an unwanted sound: I am very very sensitive to noise.

A.S.: You live in London?

J.F.: I live in London and hate it.

A.S.: Really? I live in London and love it.

J.F.: I loved it when I first came down. I was brought up in Leeds, so I am still basically a Northerner, although—if you call my bluff—

I think I am happier living in London hating it than I was living in Leeds wishing I lived in London!

A.S.: On the whole, have you been happy with the London Symphony Orchestra since you joined?

J.F.: Oh yes, I should say so. There is an atmosphere—and I do think it comes from the strings mainly—and I think this is terribly important to have a good enthusiastic corporate body of people who play as though it matters to play.

A.S.: What sort of work do you enjoy doing most of the time in London?

J.F.: Concerts: they are the most important form of music-making. I think recordings are essential—one has to spend a lot of time committing things to tape or wax, but if I had to choose one criterion by which to judge an orchestra, it would be concerts.

A.S.: It always seems to me that we never play at our best when we go away from London, even if it is just somewhere in England, but especially if it is further away, abroad. There is often a variety of reasons for this. This year in Florida, for instance, we played at less than our best . . . .

J.F.: We played atrociously in Florida; I also played atrociously in Florida.

A.S.: I think a lot of this is due to the fact that we are away from home.

J.F.: When I was in the B.B.C. we played far better on tour than we ever did in London. This is strange, isn't it?

A.S.: I don't remember the L.S.O. playing at what I felt was its best sort of standard ever, outside the Festival Hall.

J.F.: Well, heaven forbid. I think the Festival Hall acoustics bring out some of the worst qualities of the L.S.O. I am thinking of sound; it brings out the worst qualities in any orchestra. I have never liked it. Never.

I have been to lots of concerts there and there is no bloom. It's a physicist's acoustic, not a musician's acoustic at all.

A.S.: What is your taste in music now?

J.F.: To play? Very difficult; I mean, I have always loved the higher romantics. I love playing Wagner, Strauss, Mahler and Bruckner in particular.

A.S.: Do you collect records?

J.F.: I have got about 300 I should think. A lot of them are the same sort of music, purely because, I suppose, the biggest influence overall on the whole of my life has been Bruckner and Mahler, because they just happened to come into my life when I was terribly adolescent —I already knew all the Brahms and Beethoven symphonies by then and these great shattering creatures came into my life just when they

K

were needed. Nothing else has made quite the same impact on me as a musician, and, I think, as a personality.

I have always been enthusiastic about most modern music—well about a lot of it, and interested in quite a lot of the rest!

A.S.: Have you any criticism of the way music is run in London? What are the main changes you would like to see if you were running things?

J.F.: If I were running things with unlimited money there would be one orchestra less.

A.S.: Why?

J.F.: Because there are too many orchestras playing too many totally nondescript performances of good pieces.

A.S.: They are all working all the time; they are all playing to good audiences; doesn't this mean that they are needed?

J.F.: No; it means they are needed at the moment. But it is only by courtesy of the public that this situation carries on.

A.S.: Don't orchestras exist for the public?

J.F.: Yes. It depends whether you want to see four orchestras playing to seventy per cent houses or three—well, it is less than that isn't it?

A.S.: It depends on the programme. But I think that an orchestra's house is represented not only by the number of people attending a concert but by the number of people who listen to broadcasts, buy records and so on. I suppose in that sense we have better houses than orchestras have ever had in history.

J.F.: But how long is this to continue? We have got this great egalitarian philosophy which is creeping into our attitude towards culture and the money to be spent on it. There just isn't enough money for this country to live the way it is doing, so something has got to snap somewhere and the tune has got to be called. If there is a general squeeze on the middle-classes and the slightly upper middle-classes have to draw in their belts, they are not going to spend thirty bob on a seat at the Festival Hall. Or rather they will, to hear Schwarzkopf, but they won't to hear the London Symphony Orchestra doing Nielsen's Fifth; I think there is a very delicate Plimsoll Line here which could easily snap. They will very much regret not being able to afford it, but nevertheless they won't come. To this end the people who serenely point to the fact that all the orchestras are fully employed all the time are living in what could suddenly turn out to be a Fool's Paradise.

A.S.: How long has the tuba existed in the symphony orchestra?

J.F.: The first person to use the tuba was Berlioz in the Fantastic Symphony. There were one or two pretty obscure uses before this but Berlioz wrote the Fantastic Symphony for two ophicleides; the ophicleide was the forerunner of the tuba and was made of brass with keys like the big saxophone. It was really nothing more than a tuba with holes and had a brass instrument-type mouthpiece, made of wood, leading into this conical instrument. A man called Moritz discovered, or rather to some degree perfected, the tuba, which Berlioz heard and he wrote a footnote in the score of the Fantastic Symphony saying that two such instruments could be used. Moritz had been working in Berlin, in conjunction with the German Army, trying to produce a brass instrument which would make a mechanically satisfactory sound out of doors—and he came up with a version of a very very large saxhorn, which is virtually a tuba. And what exactly is a tuba?—simply a very large, wide bore horn of low pitch.

A.S.: The same as a trumpet?

J.F.: It differs from a trumpet—the trumpet is a cylindrical bore, in other words it remains cylindrical—the taper is cylindrical until suddenly it flares out into a bell. The tuba is a member of the conical bore family—the same as the cornet, flugalhorn, baritone and euphonium. They taper very much more slowly and gradually. The trombone and trumpet are the white-sounding conical instruments; the difference between the trumpet and the cornet is that the cornet is more sad—it is a blunter sound. There is this essential difference between conical instruments and straight instruments, the tuba being a conical instrument; it is a bass horn.

A.S.: Is there a scientific reason for the conical instrument's sound being more blunt or mellow, and the cylindrical one's more bright?

J.F.: It is purely an overtone structure—something that people just discovered. The posthorn, for instance, is conical; if you blow down a posthorn in an antique shop you notice that it begins to flare straight-away from the mouthpiece and it makes a surprisingly un-trumpetlike noise, although it looks like a trumpet.

A.S.: And what came before the ophicleide or tuba?

J.F.: The serpent—the serpent is a very old instrument, made of wood. But the serpent and the ophicleide have this thing in common—they have big holes in order to be able to change the pitch like a wood-wind instrument. Consequently the sound is practically nil—a very weedy, inconsequential noise. And the tuba straightaway had a relatively positive sound; it was simply a bass brass instrument.

A.S.: And what about now? Is your modern instrument the type of tuba for which Berlioz wrote?

J.F.: Well, the trouble is that various countries have taken the form of the tuba to their own laws. The Germans have always tended to use big ones—and here again we have got to distinguish between the instruments used in military bands and the instruments used in the orchestra; this is a very, very complicated subject because I don't think anyone has ever done a proper, accurate thesis on it. I certainly couldn't undertake it! But basically the Germans have always used big instruments pitched rather low; the French have always used small instruments pitched higher; the English have always used rather high instruments, too, related to the military band instruments but smaller. In this country we have always used the F tuba; nobody has ever given me an adequate explanation as to why. It certainly was used by nearly everybody here; I began to use the military instruments in the orchestra, which was a little bit bigger than the orchestral instrument which I had to use previously; it can make a very pleasant sound, but for an instrument which is supposed to provide a bass for the whole brass section, and often for the whole orchestra, I think it is totally inadequate. It is pitched in F which means that in fact most of the important bass notes are outside its range and actually played on the fourth valve—an added valve on which it is easier to get lower on notes but which is I think mechanically unsatisfactory.

A.S.: But you play an American C tuba, don't you?

J.F.: Now, yes. I was very lucky to get hold of this one; they are very dear. I got it from an American working in Vienna—he was playing in the Vienna Philharmonic Orchestra. It is a very large instrument and it has terrible problems, but if I am in good lip I think the dividend is enormous. If I am not in good lip, it is very much harder to play.

A.S.: What is the dividend? What are the advantages?

J.F.: You can get a much bigger, finer sound out of it.

Most of the other wind instruments, which are largely mechanical, have had improvements in recent years, but the tuba has lagged far behind in this respect—the trouble is that most people don't know what a tuba should sound like; they will generally accept anything that happens to come along provided it is tolerably in tune.

A.S.: Do you know what a tuba should sound like?

J.F.: Don't ask me to describe it in words. It should certainly be big and capable of making an enormous noise. I think that the tuba can be a very savage, loud, strong instrument, but most of the time it provides a big sumptuous velvet cushion for the brass section to sit on. This is how I think of it—as a velvet cushion, or a great big fat Dunlopillo mattress.

A.S.: You are married, with one brand new daughter?

J.F.: I have a brand new daughter, yes.

A.S.: And you live in London which you hate?

J.F.: Yes, let's get this, let's be fair: I don't hate it; I simply undergo periods of terror in this monstrous place. The trouble is that I am a lover of the country, of real peace and quiet, as opposed to sitting in a back garden with cars going by that you don't notice. It terrifies me that we are moving more and more towards a state of noise-unconsciousness; the ear is unfortunately very adaptable to this and you eventually get to the stage where you only notice the noise if it stops. I am terribly sensitive to noises that I don't want; my ear picks them out for an awful lot of the day. I am the sort of person who reserves the right just to be able to sit and stare into space.

A.S.: And do you have much time to do that as a musician?

J.F.: No, but I manage to create a fair amount of time. I love to be in the countryside and I love to get as far as I can into the remotest part of it. My favourite escape is just to get into the car, drive up to Yorkshire and get up on top of the moors somewhere and then I can know that there isn't another human being for five miles in all directions.

A.S.: You don't get lonely?

J.F.: No, no. I don't think there is any possibility of getting lonely in England; there are fifty million people in this tiny island and it's just not possible.

A.S.: How would you advise a young person, living away from London, who wished to play the tuba?

J.F.: I would certainly quizz him very closely as to how much he wanted to do it, and what other alternatives he had. It is a very risky business to decide that you want to become a tuba-player. There are seven orchestras in London which have a permanent tuba-player; there is perhaps enough work for three or four more to do reasonably well. This means that London can carry nine or ten tuba-players. But there are in fact more than that; they are only just scraping a living. What is more, a few years ago they were all old men, but that no longer applies; now they are all young, I think almost without exception. Apart from one or two, they are all under 40. My first advice would be to make sure that they are not wasting any other talents that they have, and I am speaking from experience now. I did a science degree which is not only an insurance against future catastrophe but also enables me to call my own bluff at any moment; musicians as a race tend to moan about their lot and to say, oh goodness, I wish I could do something else—something safe, something a bit less wearing on the nerves. If they are, say, a qualified accountant, or a qualified bank manager, they can call their own bluff and say, right, here's a job in Barclays Bank at £3,000 a year—and the chances are that they would never do it in a million years. I was trained to be a science teacher; I could walk into a perfectly good job tomorrow and it enables me to be able to say at any moment that I could push off. Consequently, I think, I enjoy it more.

It is possible, in an orchestra, to play the tuba very badly and for an awful lot of people not to know; I can't see that anyone would get any happiness out of this. I would say, if you are going to take up the tuba, that you have got to be good, both for your own benefit and for everybody else's. If you are not going to be good, somebody else is going to be better than you, and eventually someone will realise this. In a military band, or a brass band, you never play terribly loudly, never terribly softly, always in the middle of the instrument; in the symphony orchestra you have got to be the complete master of four complete octaves and the extremes of that range have been used pretty spectacularly. Berlioz certainly uses the very top octaves in such a way that you would know if you couldn't cope and similarly a number of composers have used the very low register with equal effect. I am thinking of an acquaintance of mine who wrote a cantata with a very, very bottom B flat played solo and held on for bar after bar. If you can't play it—out! In the orchestra you have got to be able to play very very loudly and very very softly—this applies to any brass instrument—and you have got to be physically fit, because the actual quantity of air which goes in and out of the lungs to do justice to many orchestral passages is absolutely colossal.

I think the main difficulty about learning the tuba is that you cannot tell how bad it sounds. There is a certain physical sensation about playing the tuba; there is a lot of vibration in the lips. It is a big instrument and you can make a room boom with the sound, and consequently it feels rather good—but in fact it usually sounds diabolical. One has got to be very critical. Another difficulty is that even with the most self-critical will in the world you really can't tell sometimes whether you are playing out of tune, or even if you are playing out of time. The trouble is again the time lag in actually producing the sound. You may feel that you are playing in a good rhythm, and in fact this sensation causes you to hear it coming out in good rhythm, whereas to an onlooker it is not at all. The semiquavers may be all too slow, or lumbered and sticky, or all that sort of thing. It is essential to have a teacher, and, of course, preferably a first class tuba player with a good ear; sometimes, of course, you can't have that. I have frequently got all sorts of people who, I think, probably have a good ear, and I have said, will you listen to this and tell me what is the matter—and they come up with the most illuminating observations.

A.S.: Tubas are rather scarce here, aren't they?

J.F.: It has always been a problem in England to get a good tuba. The only good one made in any commercial quantity in this country is the E flat bass, of which there are hundreds and hundreds, made by Boosey and Hawkes. If you want a big tuba, pitched in either C or B flat, you have got to go abroad, to Germany or America, and they cost a lot of money. There has recently been a regrettable trend in Chelsea and other wicked places, to use old, dilapidated tubas to put outside the front door and plant dahlias in; this has caused the price of dilapidated instruments to rise astronomically, which means that old instruments which play reasonably well are even more expensive and it is no longer possible to pick up a bargain on the junk stalls. At the moment one might expect to pay £150 for a reasonable secondhand tuba. Certainly, to start off on the instrument I would recommend a brass band, because most brass bands are quite well equipped with tubas and it is a very good training ground, provided that certain habits characteristic in band playing are not too drastically acquired too soon. Brass bands have evolved their own style, which is very effective for the work they do, frequently out of doors, and can enable them to play parts with technical excellence and to be able to play for an hour and a half on end, which is a sort of average band recital. It is not possible to play a tuba, as one would in the orchestra, for such a length of time. For a perfectly good grounding in the rudiments of bass playing—the bass tuba or whatever you like to call it—I would certainly recommend playing in a brass band for some period; it develops strength and stamina.

(Overleaf):
'A big sumptuous velvet cushion for
the brass section to sit on.'
John Fletcher, tuba.

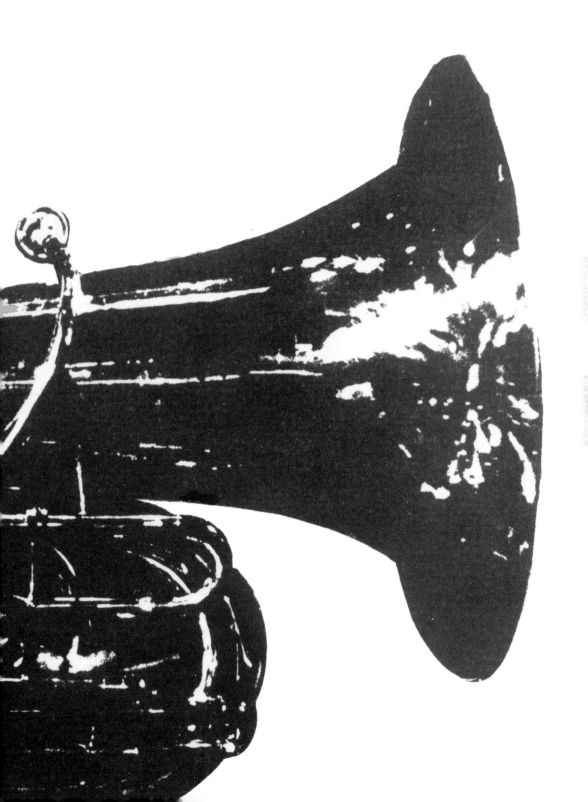

PART FIVE

The Timpani, Percussion and Harp

KURT HANS GOEDICKE
Principal Timpani

A.S.: You have been the timpani player with the L.S.O. for five years now. When did you first become aware of the timpani?

K.G.: When I first started to study music at the High School of Music in Berlin.

A.S.: You studied another instrument first?

K.G.: I started to study the clarinet, alongside of all the other compulsory things—piano, and the general musical education that you receive there. It was proposed, always, to fresh students, that they should take a secondary instrument, and I hadn't made a choice at the time, but I became aware then, in the course of the daily life inside the academy, of the percussion and timpani, to which I took a great liking. I decided to take timpani and percussions for my secondary instrument.

A.S.: Are you in fact from Germany?

K.G.: Yes, I was born in Berlin.

A.S.: And what sort of pattern did your career take from then?

K.G.: Well, we started off at the very beginning. It was my first year at the High School of Music and in my second term I had to give up the clarinet; the choice was quite obviously to switch to my secondary instrument and make that my principal instrument, so I studied—for five years in all—timpani and percussion. For another six months or a year I freelanced in Berlin and then—for reasons which I do not wish to go into now, because they really will take up too much time—I had to leave Germany altogether; as you know, I am originally from East Berlin. I had to find an appointment as a musician outside Germany and, as luck would have it, I was able to go to Ireland—to Dublin—and become principal timpanist in the Radio Eireann Symphony Orchestra. I played there for a number of years. I returned to Germany to freelance again a little, went back to Ireland and then eventually came to London. On the whole, it is rather dull.

A.S.: Well, not if it led to the L.S.O. Do you like England?

K.G.: Yes, I do, and I think of all the countries in Europe I like England in preference to any other.

A.S.: Could you describe what the timpani are—you have three kettle drums?

K.G.: Yes, the most that are played are four. Now you can play with three, with two, according to what the music demands. It is never a good idea, in my opinion, to have too many instruments standing around you when they are not used; you should limit the number of instruments to what is really necessary. A great deal, of course, depends on the player and his virtuosity.

A.S.: You can alter the note on any one kettle drum?

K.G.: Yes, you can. The range varies with the size of the drum and is peculiar to each individual drum. If you have two drums of the same size and the same type, possibly even the same manufacture, it doesn't necessarily follow that each of these drums will have exactly the same range of notes.

A.S.: How is the note altered?

K.G.: The skin or, as it's called, the head, lies flat over the rim of the kettle itself, and it is held down with a flesh hoop. The skin is firmly attached to the hoop. Over this hoop is another hoop which is called a counter hoop, and it is mechanically attached by means of screws—it is firmly attached to the centre mechanism, to the base of the instrument and, with linkages, to a pedal. When this pedal is operated either way, the counter hoop is either pulled down or released. If it is pulled down it will tighten the skin or the head evenly over the edge of the kettle, and you get a higher note, just like a string instrument—when the string is tightened it produces a higher sound; and if is it slackened, a lower sound.

A.S.: And of course you can alter the basic tension on the skin— this is what you do when you tune?

K.G.: When the head is fitted you first of all have to determine what your lowest note needs to be. You have a certain size of instrument and you must decide how low a note you need—how low a note would produce a good sound—what is the limit; you must find this limit, then put the head on and tune it to that note; it has to be tuned evenly all around the circle of the kettle, so that you have a clean note. And having tuned such a note, you then see, by using the pedal and tensioning or tightening the head, what the highest note is—and you have now determined your range.

A.S.: Is the pitch within the range infinitely variable or does it go in steps of semitones?

K.G.: It is infinitely variable.

A.S.: So you have to be quite skilful with the actual pressure on your foot if you want to play in tune?

K.G.: Yes, when you move it, say an inch—and you get to a certain stage, where let us say you have an A. You have come from the third of that below which is F. An inch on the pedal produces the A. Now as little as an eighth of an inch too little or too much will make that A very flat or very sharp. However, when you have arrived at the A you can take your foot off, and it will stay. The mechanism is devised in this way that you have freedom to take your foot off the pedal once you have operated it.

A.S.: Your instruments always look immaculate to me. Do you spend a lot of time cleaning them?

K.G.: Yes, one has to, I feel. I can't honestly see how an instrumentalist in a virtuoso orchestra like this one can afford not to look after his instrument. Not only is it his livelihood, but it is important that your instrument is always in first class working order, mechanically as well as otherwise. For how otherwise can you be expected to play well when there is something not quite in order?

A.S.: Do timpani players play other percussion instruments, or are the two things separate?

K.G.: They are not separate, at all. One must study everything, and this means that the process of studying timpani and percussion begins, or ought to begin in my opinion, with the snare drum. When you set out to become a timpanist or percussionist, or both, you start off with the snare drum, it being one of the most difficult of the percussion instruments. And then eventually when you have mastered the elementaries of this, you add on percussion instrument after percussion instrument, until eventually you have at least started them all off; eventually you come to the timpani, and so you will then have something like four major percussion instruments going at all times.

A.S.: Of course there are moments when everybody envies the timpanist; for instance, the loud interjections at the beginning of the New World Symphony, with the timpani player having a real bang there, but so much of the time you are sitting still, counting bars, and when you do play you have such a responsibility to be right, that this must call for a very special sort of self discipline and mental organisation towards the job. When you are counting bars do you allow yourself to think of other things, or are you listening to the music?

K.G.: No, I always listen to the music. Very seldom can you afford to allow yourself much freedom. Possibly you may stray a little at rehearsal, but certainly not at a concert. This can be very dangerous.

A.S.: But is it really satisfying to play an instrument like that?

K.G.: Tremendously satisfying. So much so that I can't see how anybody can play anything else. It is tremendously satisfying. It is not in fact until you play the timpani that you realise just how important it is. Play something like the first movement of Beethoven Nine, or in fact a movement from any Beethoven symphony. Well, just imagine this played minus the timpani. Beethoven uses the timpani as a harmonic instrument.

A.S.: Was there a point in history where the timpani, with a definite variable pitch, evolved from the more pitchless bass drum?

K.G.: No, there was no such point. The timpani in fact was always intended to have a pitch—a definite pitch. In fact, you know, before the timpani was ever seen in an orchestra as an orchestral instrument, there was no timpani—there was no percussion instrument added to the music other than what instruments were used in little bands and so on for effect, such as cymbals and suchlike. But then the timpani was added; one of the bass players in the orchestra would play it, because he was used to playing an instrument in this low register. This is why the German orchestras and some Continental orchestras to this day play the timpani the wrong way round. The bass player placed the timpani in front of him in such a way that the high instrument was to his left and the low instrument to his right. In other words, exactly the way his strings are placed on his bass.

A.S.: You play them here in London a different way round to the other London orchestras, don't you? Are there any practical advantages?

K.G.: I would say it is exactly the same thing really. There may be something in it when you consider that the majority of people are right-handed; it might make a difference because of this.

A.S.: As you appear at the very centre of the orchestra in a very prominent position, you give an impression of being rather unyielding and fierce. Are you?

K.G.: Not that I'm aware of! I certainly don't mean to be.

A.S.: You look very efficient.

K.G.: Well, whatever I look like, only you can tell me because I can't see myself.

A.S.: How do you manage about the mundane problem of transporting these bulky instruments?

K.G.: Well, sheer muscle, alongside with the good help of Danny Liddington, the L.S.O.'s orchestral attendant. We share the task between us.

A.S.: Are they very heavy?

K.G.: Yes indeed—the American set we have are not quite so heavy, but it still takes two people to lift one because they are awkward more than heavy. The German type of instrument that we have takes two strong men to get off the ground, and there are only two points at which the instrument should be lifted from, which means bending down in a stooped position, and then you have something like 150 pounds at least between you to get up.

A.S.: You have quite a lot of ancillary equipment, too. We always notice your array of—do you call them sticks?

K.G.: Yes, we do.

A.S.: Why is it necessary to have quite so many?

K.G.: Every pair of sticks you see on my desk is different, and they are made differently to produce different sounds. Small and slender sounds; hard sounds; medium sounds; soft sounds; sometimes sounds which no one in the orchestra is aware can come from the timpani, because that's the way they ought to sound, as just part of the general orchestral colour more than a definite timpani addition to the sound made by the rest of the orchestra. And so I find myself using a minimum of five to six pairs in every concert.

A.S.: Are there any eccentric ways of playing the timpani that occur in your repertoire?

K.G.: Well, I don't think eccentric—one plays them with wooden sticks which cut the tone quality of the instrument to a bare minimum so that it is most difficult to define the accurate pitch, but they do produce an exciting noise: brilliant and very exciting.

A.S.: Coming from Ireland and from Germany—how do you view this democratic self-governing system we have in the L.S.O.?

K.G.: I think it's wonderful. You see, it's not quite so peculiar to the L.S.O. as everybody thinks. I come from Berlin—well, there you have the Berlin Philharmonic: it governs itself, the way we do. It hasn't half the difficulties we have because they have all the money in the world, and they don't have to worry about that.

A.S.: Where do they get that from?

K.G.: I think it comes from the German Government, together with the Municipality, and their grant is, I think, twice as much as all the London orchestras get put together.

A.S.: Music has always been such a very important part of German life, hasn't it? Perhaps it hasn't always been as important as it is today in England.

K.G.: No, it hasn't. That is quite obvious from the way the profession looks at the moment.

A.S.: Do you feel that today London is a musical capital?

K.G.: I should say it is *the* musical capital of the world.

A.S.: Not Vienna?

K.G.: No, no. Vienna quite frankly in my opinion is stone dead.

A.S.: How has this come about—that London should be the centre?

K.G.: Well, I think, for one thing, the change that air travel has brought about has a lot to do with it, although this might sound very superficial—until you consider London's geographical position.

A.S.: Do you think London will continue to play this very important role in the musical world?

K.G.: It should do. If it is allowed to it will. But music, and all art, costs a lot of money, and we have to learn to accept that it is not a

L

business proposition. Money cannot be invested in art in the way that you normally invest money and expect returns.

A.S.: Well, now I would really like to ask you just about six questions in one. Let us consider the symphony orchestra as it is today: Beethoven's orchestra, roughly. Do you regard the symphony orchestra as a perfect musical art form, a completely evolved one, or do you think there will be changes taking place in the next few years that will radically alter it? What form do you think the most used orchestra will have in, say, a hundred years from now, and of what instruments will it be composed, and of how many players, and do you think it will still be professional?

K.G.: Can I have the first of those six again?

A.S.: Do you regard the symphony orchestra as we know it today as a perfectly evolved musical art form or has it any way to go?

'Music, and all art, costs a lot of money;
it is not a business proposition.'
Kurt Goedicke with Osian Ellis.

K.G.: Well, nothing is ever perfect, so perfect that it is infinite, but since you labelled it 'Beethoven's Orchestra'—yes, that is perfect.

A.S.: Do you think there will be many changes in the symphony orchestra in the next few years?—I have in mind contemporary music, electronic music, new instruments . . . do you think there will be many changes?

K.G.: New instruments, probably mechanical instruments—instruments working with electricity—computer music: yes, there will be, but I don't think they will be so readily absorbed into the symphony orchestra, as we know it, that one could speak in terms of a few years from now. They may in fact never be totally absorbed by the symphony orchestra as we understand it. They may come to form yet another way, another form of expression in musical terms, but different.

A.S.: What about the status of the musician? We are professional musicians who earn our living by playing; do you think this is an inviolate arrangement, or might this alter?

K.G.: I don't believe it will alter because the demands made by contemporary music on the orchestral musician are ever increasing, it demands more technical perfection, more virtuosity—it has done ever since Beethoven—and you must have heard, for example, of the comments of the players who were faced with the Rite of Spring when it was first performed in Paris. They couldn't play it; they just didn't have the technical equipment to play music like that. And today the Rite of Spring has been absorbed into the standard repertoire of almost every good orchestra.

A.S.: It almost became our signature tune at one point, because we seemed to be playing it nearly every week.

K.G.: It certainly is a piece that the L.S.O. plays better than any other orchestra I know. And you yourself know that music of which we give first performances is increasingly difficult from year to year; every new piece that we are asked to play has tremendous problems and becomes ever more complicated—more difficult—to play and I can't see how a non-professional musician could possibly hope ever to come anywhere close to playing this sort of music.

A.S.: The thing that worries me about the trend towards more and more difficulty and complexity in contemporary music is the fact that more and more composers who are writing—they are setting tasks for players that are not the sort of tasks that were envisaged by the designers of the instruments, sometimes producing sounds that could be produced by just tapping a piece of wood.

K.G.: Yes, this basically puts the blame on the composer, and I don't mean this in a negative sense. The composer is probably expressing the ever more complicated world in which we live, and so he resorts to an ever more complicated scoring, an ever more entangled way of writing for instruments and consequently demanding technical skills which so far we haven't been asked for.

A.S.: I realise that an individual player in the orchestra may not be the ideal judge though I think his opinions carry a lot of weight: we have just today been recording a modern contemporary French piece where a lot of the string writing was completely superfluous because it was completely drowned either by the brass or by the percussion or by an electronic organ, and it seems to me that whilst one can acknowledge that we were a thread in the texture the composer had envisaged when he wrote the notes down, this is lack of expertise, and lack of knowledge of his craft.

K.G.: But you see there are contemporary composers in this country, like Britten for instance, or like Tippett; Tippett's music is very good—and he uses the symphony orchestra as we know it today. True, he demands the extra skills I spoke of, and most of his orchestral parts are very very difficult indeed, but they do make sense, and each part belongs just where he wrote it.

A.S.: You have already said that you admire the self-governing pattern of organising a symphony orchestra, and I know from knowing you that you have a terrific pride in being a part of the L.S.O.— nevertheless, would you like to say what you like best about the L.S.O. and what you think its major faults are?

K.G.: Well, I should start with the latter half of that question first because it is quickest answered. I don't believe with all due respect to you that this is the point, the place or the time to discuss the orchestra's faults, and I would certainly not do so in a publication open to the public. You have mentioned my, as you put it, tremendous loyalty to and pride in the L.S.O. and, to affirm that statement, I would never be heard in public making any kind of comment which can be in the least detrimental to the orchestra. I would never, for example, discuss, outside the L.S.O. and outside the circle of my colleagues, its short-comings, if any.

A.S.: Perhaps organisational shortcomings, though?

K.G.: Yes, but again not outside of the orchestra. This is what we are self-governing for, and we ought to preserve that self-government very jealously because it is unique.

A.S.: Say what you like most about the L.S.O.

K.G.: Yes, of course. What I like most about it is that it is in fact so democratic. I like most, from an artistic point of view, its youthful vitality. I like the way it works, I *love* the way it plays.

JAMES HOLLAND

Principal Percussion

A.S.: How long have you been with the London Symphony Orchestra?

J.H.: Since 1962, actually.

A.S.: And you have two colleagues with you. Ray Northcott as second, and then Jack Lees who has just come from the B.B.C. Symphony. How many instruments does a percussion player in a modern symphony orchestra have to be able to play?

J.H.: That's a complicated question because there are really several groups. Some percussionists play timpani for a start. In our section I do and Ray does as well, so if there is more than one timpanist, then generally one of us will join Kurt Goedicke and play the other timpani part. Then there are tuned percussion instruments—the xylophones, vibraphone, marimba, tubular bells, glockenspiel and a number of less usual ones.

A.S.: What are the less usual ones?

J.H.: Things like crotales—little antique cymbals which you often have mounted now, laid out chromatically. Then there are things like boobams, which are like little bongo drums, but are tuned.

A.S.: *Boobams*?

J.H.: Yes, really. And then there are tuned cow bells and bell plates—all sorts of things, because percussion changes year by year. At any rate, those are the tuned percussion instruments: mainly what the Americans call the mallet instruments. Then there is the snare drum or side drum which is very much a thing of its own. Then there are all sorts of instruments which need a certain amount of skill— things like cymbals, castanets and tambourines. Then there are instruments which are purely effects, like the wood block, the whip, things like that. But, I mean, the list is inexhaustible. . . .

A.S.: So how many do you play in a year, I mean on an average; how many different instruments?

J.H.: A hundred, maybe.

A.S.: Where do you get them from?

J.H.: Well, I've got a small business for hiring instruments as well and then there's one main firm in London which does it. You see, apart from the symphony orchestras, composers are apt to dream up effects in other works, particularly if you do film sessions.

A.S.: Are you expected to play actual keyboard instruments? Do you play the piano?

J.H.: I used to, but I haven't touched it for years. On occasion I have done a few notes on the celesta, but I wouldn't count myself on that though.

A.S.: If you can't hire the instrument and you haven't got it, do you have to make it?

J.H.: That's been known, yes.

A.S.: So you have to be very well conversant in advance with what music is coming?

J.H.: Oh, yes. My mind is always working anything between three weeks and six months ahead on instruments and the number of players we require, because if we are doing a very large work we have got to get hold of a score or the parts to find out how many players, and kinds of instruments, are needed, because every concert calls for a different number of players and a different permutation of instruments.

A.S.: So there is quite a lot of office work in being a percussionist?

J.H.: A lot—a lot more than anybody realises, really.

A.S.: Does this fall mainly on the principal percussionist?

J.H.: All of it falls on the principal percussionist!

A.S.: You are responsible for the right squad being there?

J.H.: Yes, and sometimes the parts themselves take a long while to work out. Some percussion parts are written, like the Josephs that we rehearsed today. There are three percussion parts and he has got it all worked out. There is a different part for each player, so one player plays xylophone, vibraphone, cymbals, bass drum and tam tam; the second player plays marimba, bass drum and also some tam tam; the third player plays glockenspiel, whip and bass drum.

A.S.: What are the most difficult instruments to play, technically, that you encounter?

J.H.: The snare drum, side drum.

A.S.: Why is that hard?

J.H. It's very difficult to produce an even sound from it and to produce a good side drum roll.

A.S.: A side drum roll is always a sort of percussionist audition, isn't it?

J.H.: Yes, maybe. . . .

A.S.: It's more telling than a timpani roll which resounds so much.

J.H.: Yes. Because on a timpani roll the sound of the drum mixes together and helps you, whereas every tap on the side drum is alone.

A.S.: I would have thought one of your most perilous duties was the xylophone which is always heard above the full orchestra, isn't it?

J.H.: Most percussion instruments are heard; that's one of the perils of the job.

A.S.: But as a high-tuned instrument it always seems to have prominence. I mean, in the Young Person's Guide to the Orchestra by Benjamin Britten, for instance, you have those very telling few bars before the fugue—you are out on a limb there.

J.H.: Yes, percussion players are very frequently out on a limb. That's one of the things, because often you haven't got a lot to do. Often it means sitting there, you know, for twenty minutes and not doing anything at all. Then when you do play it's completely exposed.

A.S.: What do you do? What do you think about when you are sitting there for twenty minutes without anything to do?

J.H.: Listen to the orchestra playing.

A.S.: You have to keep your mind on the music and what's going on, do you feel? Is that a part of your professionalism or are you just interested, or what?

J.H.: Well, I think most players are just interested.

A.S.: What are the main pitfalls about being a percussion player? What are the main problems in performance?

J.H.: Well, thinking of a triangle for instance, if the triangle's written pianissimo on the last chord of a slow-moving movement then probably you are wrong wherever you play because the strings and wind can creep in. They more or less fall into the note, so if you play at the beginning when they start their note you sound too early because they haven't yet got there really, and if you play on the peak of the note then you sound too late, so you can't win either way! On a cymbal you can probably slide it and get in with it like that, but there are some instruments like the triangle where you can't win.

A.S.: You have to commit yourself at some point?

J.H.: Yes. It can make it very difficult when the orchestra plays a long way behind the beat too.

A.S.: Yes, I'm sure. Do you find the orchestra follows the percussion?

J.H.: Not very much, I don't think.

A.S.: I know I, on several crucial points, am aware of the percussion instruments where a conductor's beat might not be easy to follow.

J.H.: No. I think probably we are too occupied at that moment to think about it.

A.S.: I do think, however, that you percussion people do set the tempo perhaps more than you realise consciously.

J.H.: Yes, maybe.

A.S.: I know you are very busy in London even apart from the orchestra, aren't you? What sort of things do you do?

J.H.: Well, we have a percussion ensemble which David Johnson, the principal in the New Philharmonia Orchestra, and myself started. There are more difficulties in that, mainly because of moving instruments around.

A.S.: What is that, a percussion ensemble?

J.H.: Well, just a chamber group of players, but they're all percussion.

A.S.: What sort of music do you play?

J.H.: Well, there's quite a lot of stuff written now, you know, because there's so many groups—there's the Strasbourg Percussion Group which is very famous; they've done a lot with Boulez. But always you come back to the same old problem. In England you have to take your own instruments and that means so much physical work

Trumpets and trombones.

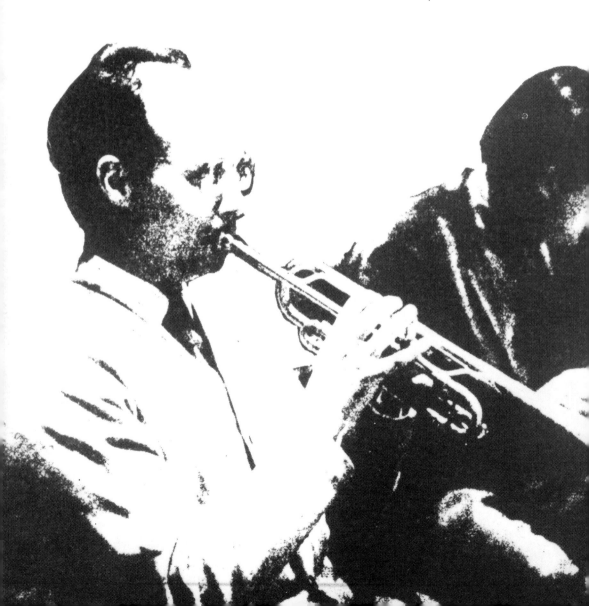

before you even start playing a note. In America, generally, if you do a session you just turn up with the more personal instruments like the side drum and the sticks and all the big stuff is there. It's all hired by the studios.

A.S.: What music does your percussion ensemble play, then? Boulez I know has written big pieces.

J.H.: Yes, there is a variety of stuff. We've had pieces written for us, and we made a long-play record about a year ago. Johnny Meyer wrote a piece for this recording which combines conventional percussion with Indian percussion instruments, which is quite interesting actually. Then of course there are percussion groups with one or two other instruments, or percussion and voice. That sort of thing.

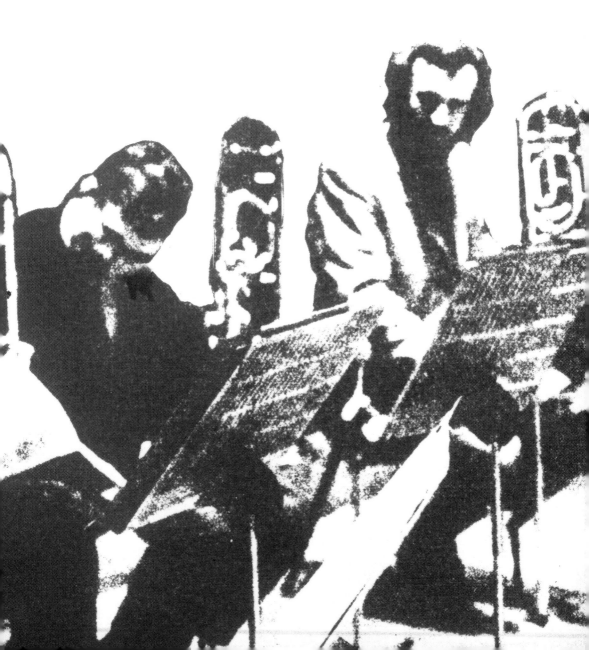

A.S.: When was the earliest 'percussion only' piece of music written?

J.H.: Must have been in the States, because percussion has been developed so much more in the States. But it is beginning to change now, because Boulez is having a lot of influence on percussion; I believe Boulez's own house is full of odd percussion instruments. American percussion has been influenced tremendously by one person in particular and that's the timpanist in the New York Phil who started there at some amazingly early age; he's been there forty years.

A.S.: So there is a high standard?

J.H.: Oh yes. Not only that, of course; all their high school bands have got better instruments than most of the symphony orchestras in London had until ten years ago.

A.S.: What is the standard of playing like in London amongst percussionists?

J.H.: Going up very quickly. It's far higher than it was when I first came, and when I joined the London Philharmonic Orchestra in 1956—sounds ridiculous now—we had equipment-wise: four hand-tuned timpani; one odd pair of cymbals, a 15-inch and a 16-inch; one tambourine with half the jingles missing; and the tam tam sounded like a dustbin lid. And that was pretty well it!

A.S.: Was that the normal order of things or had it been allowed to run down by somebody?

J.H.: Oh no, that was very little different to any of the orchestras. Now you never think of going on a session without . . . I mean the conductor says, 'Haven't you got a higher cymbal?' or a lower pitched side drum or a higher pitched one or 'Haven't you got a different bass drum?' You know. And you are expected to have all sorts of choices available on the session, which is a very different sort of scene.

A.S.: Yes. I had thought, watching you dealing diplomatically with conductors, that you do have to school yourself to shrug and always be in the wrong. Because it's very easy for a conductor to say that's not quite . . .

J.H.: Well, they arrive with a preconceived idea in their minds. Percussion instruments, cymbals for instance and side drums, it's very much a matter of what your ear is used to hearing so they will always tend to ask for the sort of sound that they are used to hearing in their own orchestras.

(Top): Percussionists David Johnson, Michael Fry, Ray Northcott and Jack Lees in conference with timpanist Kurt Goedicke (second from right). ▶
(Bottom): David Johnson, Ray Northcott, Michael Fry and Jack Lees, percussions.

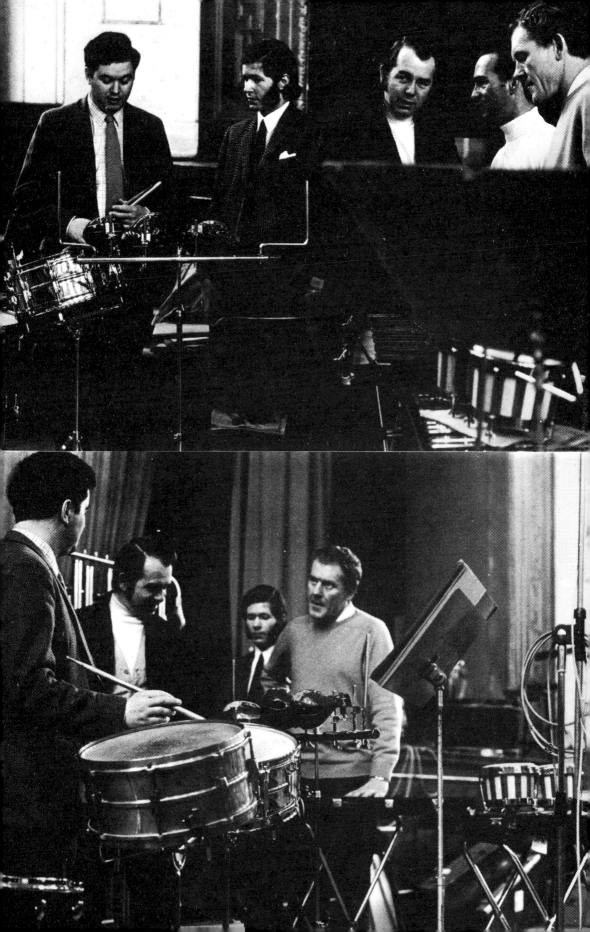

A.S.: You do film work and pop sessions?

J.H.: Yes—very few pop sessions for me personally.

A.S.: That's mostly a different kind of percussionist, is it?

J.H.: Yes, really, but I do the odd one or two.

A.S.: And your percussion ensemble: I suppose there is some percussion in chamber music?

J.H.: Oh yes, quite a lot, increasingly. I enjoy that too.

A.S.: Would you have much time for anything else?

J.H.: Not enough, at any rate. I live in Buckinghamshire at the back
of Pinewood Studios, which is a fair way out, but on the other hand it
faces out over acres of woods. It's very pleasant.

A.S.: As principal percussion you are also responsible for delegating
the various instruments to the various players for any performance.

J.H.: The nature of percussion being as it is you never find
any player who is brilliant at everything, so I have my own
personal assessment of everybody's abilities and work the parts out
accordingly.

A.S.: What do you base your assessment on?

J.H.: Well, my personal experience of them.

A.S.: You don't audition them?

J.H.: No, percussion auditions are—I don't really like them at all.

A.S.: You have to see how people behave actually in a concert
condition?

J.H.: Yes, because on percussion you find that people can do it all
marvellously in the room at the back of the stage, but when it comes to
doing it in context, doing it with the orchestra, they just don't make it
at all.

A.S.: Apart from the interest of having all these lovely instruments,
toys to play with, the interest of dealing with all the personnel and
arranging for the right instruments—and I can see that that would all
be very absorbing—what are the main musical rewards of doing what
you do?

J.H.: That's a difficult question; I wouldn't know how to put it in
words, but there's certainly plenty of music, you know—you get your
kicks out of it musically, for sure.

A.S.: You see, Stuart Knussen, our principal bass, said once that he
got his musical kicks mainly out of other people's playing. Would that
apply to your department?

J.H.: Sometimes, yes, for sure. I mean, if we are doing Brahms Four
and I've got to sit there and just play the triangle I feel a fool, quite
honestly, when the orchestra stands up to take its bow at the end,
because I—you know. I hate doing those pieces.

A.S.: But it's a very telling triangle part in Brahms Four.

J.H.: Yes, but it's just sitting there and just playing the triangle I suppose.

A.S.: And what is it like as a career being a London percussion player? Is it financially secure?

J.H.: Oh yes, I think so definitely; you know, it's like any other instrument, you've got to have the breaks. You have got to have the ability, obviously, and then you have just got to have the luck.

A.S.: What about the competition in London?

J.H.: Well, there's plenty of competition. I think the number of players always finds its own level because either you are going to get enough work out of it to make a decent living or else you turn to something else.

A.S.: You've got to have initiative, haven't you, on any percussion instrument?

J.H.: Oh, definitely yes.

A.S.: I think that's the main impression I have; one of initiative and commitment and courage.

J.H.: Yes, and the ability to do half a dozen things at the same time and to be able to turn round and change sticks and change parts. You might, in a complicated time—a complicated set of bars, time-wise— you might have to move over two or three different music stands.

A.S.: Without knocking them over.

J.H.: Well, you've got to hold it all in your mind as you go from one to the other.

A.S.: Yes, it calls for some pretty deft footwork, I suppose!

Now, as a non-director, shareholder of the orchestra do you feel you have enough voice in its affairs, or do you ever feel that the direction, the pace of the orchestra is out of your hands?

J.H.: No. Generally I think we have our say. If we feel very strongly about any one thing we can very quickly and easily call a special meeting. I would like to think that the ordinary voter in the country had as much power over the government as we do over the Board of Directors.

OSIAN ELLIS

Principal Harp

A.S.: The London Symphony Orchestra has many very distinguished solo players, not the least of whom is Doctor Osian Ellis, our principal harpist. As well as your career with the L.S.O., you have a lot of activities outside the orchestra, don't you?

O.E.: One usually has a very busy schedule with recitals all over the place—this country and abroad—and also chamber music; I play with the Melos Ensemble and I play a lot with Benjamin Britten in his church operas, which involves a small group of players. I do a lot of recording with other orchestras, other than the L.S.O., so I seem to have very little free time. Fortunately the L.S.O. have been very charitable towards me and they let me be away in order to fulfil some of these other engagements.

A.S.: What happens when you are away, how is the harp gap filled?

O.E.: We have been very fortunate in the L.S.O. in this respect, with Renata Scheffel-Stein, who is the principal harpist with the New Philharmonia Orchestra.

As you know, very often an orchestra doesn't use a harp, if they are playing Mozart or Beethoven or Brahms, so when the Philharmonia is playing, under Klemperer, Beethoven or Mozart, then she is not working and she is able to do the work I am not able to do here, which is very useful.

A.S.: You do quite a lot of lecture recitals and talking about the harp?

O.E.: Yes, I do, especially if I go to schools; if one has a young audience, one turns one's recitals into more informal affairs and talks about the harp, which is quite an interesting piece of machinery.

A.S.: I wonder if you could give us a bit of that.

O.E.: Well, let's start with the bow and arrow—the early huntsman strummed his string, and it made a musical sound apart from throwing an arrow into the air. He turned this into a musical instrument with more strings, and put on a sound board, and so on, and the harp evolved through many ages, and is found in some way or another in nearly all civilisations; in our time the harp has developed by mechanical means as well. So, on the normal harp we have 46 strings. Each string is different, a very short and thin string at the top and then, as you come lower down the scale, thicker and longer, until you have thick strings at the bottom of the harp. Most of the strings are made of gut; occasionally one can use nylon strings, particularly in hot humid climates because it doesn't react as badly as gut does; but for the bottom of the harp, we change over to wire strings. Then we have pedals at the bottom of the harp, nothing like pedals on the piano; there are seven pedals on the harp. You have got the equivalent of the white notes on the piano scale of C major and there is a pedal for each of these seven notes in the scale. On every string of a harp you have three sounds, a flat, a natural and a sharp, and you set your pedals to correspond to whatever key you are going to play in. The pedals are in the natural position like the white notes of a piano when they are in the middle position, so if you are going to play in C major you have all your pedals in the middle; but if you play in A flat major you need four flats, so you set your pedals to correspond to that key. Then, of course, when you play the music you have changes of key all the time, chromatic notes, or accidentals as they are called. Then your feet and the pedals will have to move sometimes quite furiously in order to get the right notes on the strings of the harp. That's the basic principle of the harp which has only really been finalised in the last 150 years. The harp has hardly been changed from when it was perfected by Sebastien Erard in Paris in about 1810. Before that they had simpler and cruder forms of harp for which Carl Philipp Emanuel Bach and Mozart wrote. Handel wrote for the harp, but he wrote for a different sort of harp again—one with three rows of strings called a Welsh or triple harp, which is a very difficult instrument to play and has now become pretty well obsolete. As I said, Sebastien Erard perfected the harp mechanism and gave us a full range of keys, and after that time most composers took some interest in it; you got people like Berlioz and Wagner writing for it. Berlioz used twelve harps in his Te Deum and Wagner used six to get his 'heavenly music' at the end of an opera. In France there was a long vogue for the harp; Debussy and Ravel wrote a lot for it—using two or three harps in an orchestra. But we haven't a great deal of solo music, though there was a lot of rubbish written for the harp in the nineteenth century, just as there was for the guitar; one doesn't want to hear a great deal of this. The most memorable music perhaps is that written by Ravel, his Introduction and Allegro for harp with string quartet, flute and clarinet. There is a wonderful piece by Debussy, Sacred and Profane Dances, for harp and string orchestra. Then in our own time Benjamin Britten has written a lot for the harp in his operas, in his orchestral scores, and this year he wrote a piece for me which is in five movements, a sort of classical suite for harp.

A.S.: You're a personal friend of his by now, surely, after all these Aldeburgh Festivals and other collaborations with him?

O.E.: Well, I pride myself on knowing him quite well, and it is a marvellous privilege to know a composer and artist of his calibre and to have somebody like that writing for you. Then there is quite a lot for the harp in his church operas; these are like church parables, almost like medieval plays performed in churches. There is Curlew River, his first opera; then came the Burning Fiery Furnace; and then the Prodigal Son. They are written for a small group of instruments, chamber organ, flute, viola, horn, double bass, percussion and harp—these are lovely little operas and he uses a harp a great deal.

A.S.: What is it you admire most about Britten's music?

O.E.: I think his music has a great deal of humanity, which is lacking in much of the music today. Music has changed a great deal in our time and this is one thing I find lacking. I find Britten's music also includes for me a spiritual quality which I find very elusive these days from other composers. He is one of the few religious composers of our time, and that I admire.

A.S.: It is often said he is not an avant-garde composer, in fact his techniques, in the mainstream, are almost old-fashioned.

O.E.: Conservative in some sense, yes. But I think he also has tremendous imagination and because he is not in the class of music which we call avant-garde I think it is a mistake to think he is not advanced. His techniques in the church operas are quite difficult and also in the cello symphonies there is a tremendous freedom of expression.

A.S.: Do you think this music will still be around in fifty years?

O.E.: I am definitely sure of it.

A.S.: More practically talking about the harp: it is quite a job keeping four strings in serviceable condition, but you have got forty-seven.

O.E.: Forty-six or forty-seven depending on the harp I use.

A.S.: It must be a bit of a nightmare in hot climates, or under hot television lights, or even just in a hot concert hall atmosphere, keeping them serviceable and in tune?

O.E.: Yes, the gut strings are very sensitive to the atmosphere; not so much to heat and cold, but to the amount of humidity, to the amount of dampness in the air, and one has to keep tuning all the time and anticipate what is going to happen during a concert. I don't tune a harp much before a concert; I often see harpists going to a concert half an hour before, and by the time the orchestra has come on, the audience has arrived and the lights have been switched on, the whole temperature has changed. The whole tuning process has been wasted therefore, so I prefer to wait until the orchestra is about to come on and then tune very quickly.

A.S.: I think you are unique amongst the harpists I know in that you come on virtually at the last minute to tune your harp. I remember when we had a local player in Chicago at Ravinia Park, she was on the platform tuning the harp about twenty minutes before and then, panic stricken, asked: 'Where is Mr Ellis; why is he not tuning his harp?' You seemed rather less concerned than she did.

O.E.: I think this is the reason; I don't see much point in tuning the harp before the time of the concert.

A.S.: The harp is a most beautiful instrument with one of the loveliest tone colours in the orchestra. A lot of young people would like the idea of playing the harp but they are very scarce and expensive instruments to find.

O.E.: The old harps which we play in this country are mostly Erard harps, from the same factory of Sebastien Erard; he brought his factory to London and made harps here. Well, those are the harps which have been used in this country for many many years and it's only in the last decade that we have been importing new harps. There are one or two very good harps. The Americans have made very good harps, Loud and Healey, Wurlitzer harps. Harps are now coming in from Germany, Obermeyer harps, and more recently from an Italian harp-maker called Saldi—who has opened a shop in London, which is a very good thing. Only the other day I telephoned the shop saying I wanted to come in for some strings and the man said 'I have got four harps to sell today so I am going to be a rather busy salesman this week'. When I arrived at the shop three hours later, he had already sold all four harps.

A.S.: If someone came to you for a consultation, would you be able to tell them whether they had an aptitude for the harp?

O.E.: First they would need a background of piano playing—purely for convenience because the piano is much easier, all the notes are right there in front of you—and reading music is also much easier. I encourage small students to begin with the piano and then come to the harp which has all the strings close to your face. If you learn to play without looking, so much the better; it takes a long long time and the margin of error on the harp is twice as much as the piano. There is maybe an inch between two fingers on a piano keyboard, between the two notes; but on a harp there is only half an inch between two strings.

A.S.: Also the piano has black and white notes; but you only have the odd coloured string. What does this indicate?

O.E.: We have coloured strings to find our way around. Our C strings are red and the F strings are blue or black and the rest are colourless in between.

A.S.: It is a beautiful instrument and you obviously have a fascinating

M

life playing it; why then discourage a person from playing the harp?

O.E.: Because of the difficulties of getting around with the harp! A harp weighs nearly a hundredweight if you carry it around with just a canvas cover. But if you carry it around in a box for its protection it weighs twice as much as that, so a young lady who has to get around the country with it is taking something on, I think, when she decides to play a harp. You have to drive to almost every engagement and you need a decent-sized car; when you get there, you have to get the harp into the building and on to the platform; and when the concert is over you have to pack it up again. It is much heavier than a double bass.

A.S.: Is it any good at all for a student to start on the small Celtic harp?

O.E.: Yes, I would advise that anyway for a young child. Certainly before buying a large harp you should get hold of a small Irish harp—or clarsach harp as they are called. The clarsach harp stands about 2 feet 6 to 3 feet high. You can play it sitting on a small stool. It is not chromatic—it is a diatonic instrument, but you can change some of the notes with a little blade which comes into operation at the top of each string. Still, you can play quite a lot of music and often with a young child of eight or ten, who wants to play the harp, I would advise them to take that instrument up and get a larger harp later on, when they have really got over the initial difficulties.

A.S.: How did you start on the harp?

O.E.: We had a harp at home; my mother played and we all used to sing or play the piano. I used to play the organ as a child.

A.S.: Were you a big family?

O.E.: We were a family of four children—two boys, two girls—and we used to give concerts in churches and chapels and so on. Somehow, music-making is a more natural thing in Wales; it is more normal Musicians and poets are part of the society, whereas in England musicians and poets are traditionally oddities, not of the society, which is rather sad. Maybe we can change this before long.

I used to play football at school and was probably better at it than the harp—I enjoyed it more. But being a musician at an early age was quite a normal thing. I think that now-a-days it is less of an oddity here, because of our Youth Orchestras and so on, and musician-shaping in young people is more encouraged whereas twenty or thirty years ago it wasn't.

A.S.: With that sort of atmosphere in Wales, why is it that you are based in London?

◄ *'Quite an interesting piece of machinery.'*
Osian Ellis, harp.

O.E.: I think that one of the best places for music in the world is in London. It is a very fine musical centre and there are more musical activities here than any other capital in Europe.

A.S.: It is regrettable though that music is so centralised in London.

O.E.: We need much more devolution into other parts of the country. People in the country are getting tired of so much central government.

A.S.: And how could that be done with music?

O.E.: It means that centralization must stop, in all forms of life, in Parliament and in the Civil Service; they must be centred all around the country. One could imagine federalization in certain small ways and music must develop the same way. I think it will happen—we have in Manchester a very good centre for music, a very lively centre. Liverpool also has quite a lot of activity and also Glasgow and Edinburgh. Swansea has its festival, but that lasts for a week or so and that is their lot of good music for the year. This is a pity. There is not enough cause for music and this is partly their own fault and partly the fact that so many people have fled to London from other parts of the country.

A.S.: Do you think that the London-based orchestras could do more to help this situation?

O.E.: I think that many of the orchestras are already doing a lot in Wales already—they give a lot of concerts down there. No, I think the problem is the audiences; I think we haven't got sufficient good audiences to make employment for a whole orchestra down there.

A.S.: Why is that? Wales is a very musical country; can't they provide an audience for Welsh opera? Actually, the Swansea Festival was by no means sold out when we last went there.

O.E.: No, this is where I find the audiences really are at fault as they prefer to sit at home and watch television. They have lost so many of their choral societies which used to flourish at one time. But there is much depopulation in Wales and Central England, and most people come to the south. There is your potential intelligent audience; we have lost them from their original native parts and that is the pity.

A.S.: There are no signs of devolution at the moment?

O.E.: No, not yet; there is activity on the part of nationalists and so on to encourage more devolution. It may come eventually because the Government is off balance in London and very unwieldy.

A.S.: I know you are married and have a family. How many children have you?

O.E.: I have two boys. They are about ten and thirteen; they are both singing in the Queen Elizabeth Hall today in an opera by Benjamin Britten—they sing in the Finchley Opera Group.

A.S.: Do either of your boys play the harp?

O.E.: No, they haven't really shown an interest in the harp. The two boys are rather independent, though I think they like music. The older boy is more interested in pop at the moment, and the younger boy shows quite a lot of talent—he likes singing. They both play the violin. I would encourage them to take up music, but if they don't really want to do so, then I shan't. I can push the younger one, perhaps, because he shows much more musicianship and more excitement with music—so maybe I can do something with him.

A.S.: Is your wife a musician?

O.E.: Yes, we were students together. She plays the viola, but she had to give it up naturally because she gives her attention to her husband and children.

A.S.: And what about your attention to your family? Is there any time left after your professional life for them?

O.E.: Yes, I think I find quite a lot of time for them, and occasionally I take them abroad with me. They have managed to come with me to America for the Daytona Festival on four occasions. They came with me to France and Denmark when I was doing a concert tour there; we have all been to Switzerland and Germany when we have played there. Occasionally my wife comes with me and we share the driving. Sometimes when I have gone with the Melos Ensemble we have had to go to Italy and Yugoslavia which means driving all the way to Venice, which is 1,000 miles, doing a couple of concerts there, going over to another festival at Zagreb, doing a couple of concerts there, and then driving back again through Austria and Germany, which is a tremendous amount of driving just for one or two concerts. And my income tax man wonders why I haven't made any profits on these concerts! I take a long time explaining that sometimes we do chamber music for very little reward.

A.S.: What is your favourite musical activity?

O.E.: I enjoy all the activities. I suppose I could live by just doing solo recitals and I often feel I am doing enough work for two or three people; but I find that if one lives just in recitals by oneself all the time one gets a very one-sided view of life—a lonely view. I get an elation and pleasure out of being in a large group, apart from the actual playing of large orchestral scores, where your canvas is so much larger; you work with such fine conductors as the L.S.O. works with and this gives you an extra advantage on those people who just play by themselves.

A.S.: What about when you are not playing, do you have any other interests or hobbies?

O.E.: I play football with the boys at home sometimes. I enjoy swimming when that is convenient and I have a cottage up in North

Wales. I try and get there when I can. There I have a mill and a smithy so there is a lot of work I can do there—and a lot of gardening.

A.S.: Do you keep a harp there?

O.E.: No—I get away from the harp.

A.S.: Would you say what you like most about being a professional harpist?

O.E.: That is a difficult question, because very often I feel I could give it up because it is quite a hard life. Maybe it is because I am doing too much.

A.S.: Is it nerve-racking?

O.E.: Yes, it is. Another strange thing is that sometimes I can come back to this orchestra and be petrified about playing some little pieces and yet when I was sitting in front of an audience by myself doing a whole concerto or a whole recital I won't have had these nervous feelings.

A.S.: How do you cope with it?

O.E.: I think maybe one is not as strong physically as one should be occasionally. The only way to really cope is when you are on top of the world; if you are below your one hundred per cent, then you have difficulty. Sometimes it depends on the conductor; he can make it difficult or easy for you. You enjoy playing something sometimes and on another day you might be quite nervous with the same tune. This is quite curious: something of which I have never been quite able to assess the cause. But it is something a musician, or an actor, must live with.

A.S.: Something that goes with temperament, sensitivity, perhaps even intelligence?

O.E.: Yes, I suppose it has something to do with that. Some people are more aware of their thoughts than others and some people seem to feel things quite calmly, yet you are not quite sure they are as calm as they appear. People say to me: 'Did you have nerves because you look so all right.' I do try to look as if I am enjoying myself; that is one way of making music and one attitude to have. Although you may have qualms about giving a performance, the best way is to say: 'Here it is, let's hope it will be all right!'

'All I can say is that I am very happy.'
Alex Taylor, viola. ▶

...ony Orchestra

...tes
...liam Bennett
...er Lloyd
...vry Sanders
...hard Taylor

...colo
...vry Sanders

...oes
...er Lord
...hony Camden
...ry Lythell

...r Anglais
...hony Camden

...rinets
...vase de Peyer
...y Jowitt
...nald Moore
...e Hambleton

...lat Clarinet
...nald Moore

Bass Clarinet
Hale Hambleton

Bassoons
Roger Birnstingl
Peter Francis
Patrick Milne

Contra Bassoon
Peter Francis

Horns
Ivan David Gray
Anthony Halstead
James Quaife
Martin Shillito
Peter Civil

Trumpets
William Lang
Howard Snell
George Reynolds
Norman Archibald
Laurence Evans

Trombones
Denis Wick
Peter Gane

Bass Trombone
Frank Mathison

Tuba
John Fletcher

Timpani
Kurt-Hans Goedicke

Percussion
James Holland
Ray Northcott
John Lees

Harp
Osian Ellis
Renata Scheffel-Stein

Piano
Robert Noble

Orchestral Attendant
Donald Liddington

ADMINISTRATION

Board of Directors
Stuart Knussen *Chairman*
Ronald Moore *Vice-Chairman*
Paul Katz
Peter Lloyd
Jack Long
Howard Snell
Alan Smyth
John Fletcher
Sydney Colter

General Manager
Harold Lawrence

Secretary
Alan Fabes, F.C.A.

Concerts Manager
Sue Mallet

Assistant to the General Manager
Christine Johnson

Librarian
Henry Greenwood

Personnel Manager
Terence Palmer

Assistant
Stephen Rumsey

INDEX

The page numbers in *italic* refer to illustrations.

A

Abbado, Claudio, 43
Aldeburgh Festival, 176
Arrau, Claudio, 58
Artis, Samuel, 47–50, *72–73*
Arts Council of Great Britain, 11, 76, 127

B

Bach, C. P. E., 175
Bach, J. S., 16, 45, 79, 80, 103, 138
Bach, Vincent (trumpets), 126
Barbirolli, Sir John, 14, 29
Barshai, Rudolf, 14
Bath Festival Orchestra, 39
B.B.C. Symphony Orchestra, 109, 145, 165
Beatles, 74
Beecham, Sir Thomas, 29
Beethoven, Ludwig van, 20, 46, 52, 53, 66, 71, 74, 83, 85, 92, 93, 108, 122, 135, 140, 145, 159, 163, 174
Beinum, Eduard van, 83
Benge (trumpets), 126
Benham, William, 37–46
Bennett, William, 79
Berg, Alban, 46
Berio, Luciano, 135
Berlin High School of Music, 157
Berlin Philharmonic Orchestra, 49, 81, 161
Berlioz, Hector, 49, 59, 76, 131, 146–147, 150, 175
Bernstein, Leonard, 17
Birmingham, City of, Symphony Orchestra, 28, 129, 140
Birnstingl, Roger, 99–109, *101*
Black, Cilla, 31
Boehm, Theobald, 80
Boosey and Hawkes, 91, 131, 132, 150
Borsdorf, Adolf, 8
Boston Symphony Orchestra, 13, 16, 19
Boulez, Pierre, 46, 100, 168, 169, 170
Brahms, J., 20, 37, 46, 58, 82, 91, 145, 172, 174

Brain, Denis, 116
Britten, Benjamin, 21, 135, 164, 167, 174, 175, 176, 180
Brown, John, 10, *24–25*
Bruckner, Anton, 130, 145
Burney, Charles, 130
Busby, Thomas R., 8

C

Camden, Anthony, 10
Camden, Archie, 71
Carnegie Hall, 20, 113
Casals, Pablo, 65–66
Chopin, Frederic, 17
Civil, Alan, 143
Cleghorn, Arthur, 71
Cliburn, Van, 17
Coates, Eric, 16
Copland, Aaron, 21, 51
Covent Garden Orchestra, 66
Cruft, John, 76
Cummings, Douglas, 58–62, *61*
Curtis Institute, Philadelphia, 118

D

Danzi, Franz, 108
Davis, Colin, 43
Daytona Beach Festival, Florida, 113, 181
Debussy, Claude, 86, 175
Dittersdorf, Carl Ditters von, 69
Dorati, Antal, 129, 131
Drury Lane Theatre Orchestra, 39
Duffy, John, *18*
Dugarde, Harry, 76
Dvorak, Antonin, 59, 67, 118

E

Elgar, Sir Edward, 9, 53, 59
Ellis, Dr. Osian, *162*, 174–182, *178*
Erard, Sebastien, 175, 177

F

Fleischman, Ernest, 87
Fletcher, John 143–151, *152–153*
Florida International Music Festival,
    Daytona Beach: *see under*
    Daytona Beach
Francis, Peter, *107*
Fry, Michael, *171*
Furtwängler, Wilhelm, 50

G

Gane, Peter, 10
Georgiadis, John, 10, *15, 24–25,* 26–37
Gershwin, George, 58
Gilbert, Geoffrey, 81
Glazunov, Alexander, 52
Goedicke, Kurt Hans, 157–164, *162,* 165,
    171
Goossens, Leon, 71
Gough, Christopher, 67
Gray, Ivan David, 10, 113–123, *120–121*
Greensmith, Harold, 141
Greenwood, Henry, 11
Guadagnini, Lorenzo, 34
Guildhall School of Music, 81, 134

H

Hallé Orchestra, 81
Halstead, Anthony, 10
Hambleton, Hale, 10
Handel, G. F., 175
Haydn, Josef, 16, 20, 53, 92
Heifetz, Jascha, 45
Hindemith, Paul, 116
Holland, James, 165–172
Hooley, Patrick, *56–57*
Horenstein, Jascha, 59
Houston Symphony Orchestra, 14

J

Jacob, Gordon, 134
Jaffa, Max, 66
Johnson, David, 167, *171*
Jones Hall, Houston, 20
Josephs, Wilfred, 166
Jowitt, Roy, 95, 98

K

Kanga, Homi, 38, 39, 42, 46
Karajan, Herbert von, 99

Kell, Reginald, 71
Kennedy, Thomas, 65
Kertesz, Istvan, 9
Kingsway Hall, 67
Kleiber, Erich, 66
Klemperer, Dr. Otto, 174
Knussen, Stuart, 68–76, *75,* 144, 172
Krips, Joseph, 9

L

Lalo, Edouard, 43
Lang, William, 10
Lawrence, Harold, 11
Lees, Jack, 165, *171*
Liddington, Danny, 11, 160
Lloyd, Peter, 79–81, *88–89*
London Mozart Players, 62
London Orchestral Concerts Board, 11
London Philharmonic Orchestra, 33, 50,
    51, 54, 55, 63, 170
Long, Jack, 63–66, *64*
L.S.O. Club, 11, 12, 142
L.S.O. Trust, 11
Lord, Roger, 76, 82–86, *84, 86*
Los Angeles Music Centre, 20
Loud and Healey (harps), 177
Loveday, Alan, 45
Lythell, Harry, *86*

M

Magini, 70
Mahler, Gustav, 20, 58, 59, 79, 135, 145
Manchester College of Music, 67, 81
Mathis, Johnny, 31
Mathison, Frank, 140–143
McGee, Andrew, 46
McGee, Robin, *18*
McGuire, Hugh, 48, 76
Measham, David, *24–25*
Meerschen, H. van der, 8
Melos Ensemble, 174, 181
Mendelssohn-Bartholdy, Felix, 21
Meyer, Johnny, 169
Monteux, Pierre, 9, 82
Monteverdi, Claudio, 71
Moore, Ronald, 94–98, *97*
Moritz, 147
Mozart, W. A., 10, 37, 45, 53, 58, 59, 69,
    85, 90, 91, 92, 103, 116, 122, 135,
    140, 174, 175
Muscant, Peter, 67
Musical Education, 16–19, 34, 47–48,
    63, 66–67, 70, 74, 123

N

National Youth Orchestra of Great Britain, 37
New Philharmonia Orchestra, 99, 168, 174
New York Philharmonic Orchestra, 16, 170
Nielsen, Carl, 146
Nikisch, Arthur, 9
Northcott, Ray, 165, *171*
Northern Symphony Orchestra, B.B.C., 81

O

Obermeyer (harps), 177
Oldham, Arthur, 12
Ormandy, Eugene, 14

P

Palmer, Terry, 10, 11
Peter Stuyvesant Foundation, 11
Peyer, Gervase de, 76, 82, 87–94, 95, 98
(Philadelphia) Academy of Music, 20
Philadelphia Orchestra, 13, 14, 16
Philomusica of London, 67
Piatigorsky, Gregor, 59, 65
Plomley, Roy, 16
Pougnet, Jean, 37, 38
Previn, Andre, 9, 13–21, *15*, *18*, 28, 32, 34, 43, 44, 45, 50, 58, 59, 143

Q

Quantz, Johann Joachim, 79, 80
Queen Elizabeth Hall, 20, 180
Queen's Hall, 9
Queen's Hall Orchestra, 8

R

Rachmaninov, Sergei, 50, 92
Radio Eireann Symphony Orchestra, 157
Ravel, Maurice, 175
Ravinia Park, Chicago, 177
Redfield, John, 19
Richter, Hans, 8, 9
Robinson, Martin, *64*, 66–68
Rodney Bennett, Richard, 28
Rolling Stones, The, 17
Rowicki, Witold, 36

Royal Academy of Music, 30, 65, 66, 67, 123
Royal Albert Hall, 11, 49, 92, 93, 102
Royal Festival Hall, 19, 20, 47, 55, 67, 106, 145, 146
Rozhdestvensky, Gennady, 43, 96
Rumsey, Stephen, 11

S

Sadlers Wells Opera, 66, 67
Saldi (harps), 177
Sargent, Sir Malcolm, 93
Saunders, Lowry, 10
Sax, Adolph, 130–131
Scheffel-Stein, Renata, 174
Schoenberg, Arnold, 46, 71, 135
Schubert, Franz, 116, 135
Schumann, Robert, 52, 59
Schwarzkopf, Elisabeth, 146
Scottish National Orchestra, 81
Sibelius, Jean, 21, 135
Sinfonia of London, 87
Smyth, Alan, *56–57*
Snell, Howard, 10, 123–128, *136–137*
Solomon, John, 8
Stamitz, Family, 52
Stern, Isaac, 85
Stokowski, Leopold, 36, 37, 129
Stratton, George, 48
Strauss, Richard, 32, 71, 116, 135, 145
Stravinsky, Igor, 102
Stringer, Alan, 123
Swansea Festival, 180
Szell, George, 27, 29, 43

T

Taylor, Alexander, 51–55, *183*
Tchaikovsky, Peter, 118, 129
Tchaikovsky Violin Competition, 39
Telemann, Georg, 52
Tertis, Lionel, 51–52
Three Choirs Festival, 48
Thurston, Frederick, 71
Tippett, Sir Michael, 21, 164
Trevanni, Francesco, 52
Tuckwell, Barry, 76, 142, 143

V

Vaughan Williams, Dr. Ralph, 50, 53
Vella, Oliver, 67

Verdi, Giuseppe, 103
Vienna Philharmonic Orchestra, 16, 148
Vivaldi, Antonio, 108

W

Wagner, Richard, 130, 135, 145, 175
Walton, Sir William, 21, 28, 59

Weber, Carl Maria von, 90, 108
Webern, Anton [von], 17, 46
Wick, Denis, 10, 129–139, *133*
Wigmore Hall, 106
Wood, Sir Henry, 8
Worthing Municipal Orchestra, 38
Wurlitzer (harps), 177